Hiking Death Valley National Park

National Park

36 Day and Overnight Hikes

Bill and Polly Cunningham

FALCONGUIDES ®

GUILFORD, CONNECTICUT
HELENA, MONTANA
AN IMPRINT OF THE GLOBE PEQUOT PRESS

FALCONGUIDES®

Text design by Nancy Freeborn
Maps created by XNR Productions Inc. © Morris Book Publishing, LLC
All interior photos by Polly and Bill Cunningham

Library of Congress Cataloging-in-Publication Data is available.

ISBN 978-0-7627-4463-3

Manufactured in the United States of America
First Edition/Second Printing

To buy books in quantity for corporate use
or incentives, call **(800) 962–0973**
or e-mail **premiums@GlobePequot.com.**

The authors and The Globe Pequot Press assume no liability for accidents happening to, or injuries sustained by, readers who engage in the activities described in this book.

To the thousands of citizens from California and elsewhere, past and present, who laid the groundwork for protection of a large portion of the California desert and to the dedicated state and federal park rangers and naturalists charged with stewardship of California's irreplaceable desert wilderness.

Help Us Keep This Guide Up to Date

Every effort has been made by the authors and editors to make this guide as accurate and useful as possible. However, many things can change after a guide is published—trails are rerouted, regulations change, techniques evolve, facilities come under new management, etc.

We welcome your comments concerning your experiences with this guide and how you feel it could be improved and kept up to date. While we may not be able to respond to all comments and suggestions, we'll take them to heart, and we'll also make certain to share them with the authors. Please send your comments and suggestions to the following address:

The Globe Pequot Press
Reader Response/Editorial Department
P.O. Box 480
Guilford, CT 06437

Or you may e-mail us at:

editorial@GlobePequot.com

Thanks for your input, and happy trails!

Contents

Acknowledgments

This book could not have been written without the generous assistance from knowledgeable park staff. Special thanks to Charlie Callagan, interpretative ranger and still one of the leading authorities on wilderness hiking in Death Valley. Charlie is now on the permanent ranger staff for Death Valley National Park. He is a virtual fountain of information and enthusiasm for the park. He provided an in-depth review of our draft material time and again until he was satisfied that we finally had it right. But most of all, Charlie served as friend and guide on several of the hikes, notably South Fork Hanaupah and Upper Hole-in-the-Wall.

Thanks also to Esy Fields, director of the Death Valley Natural History Association. And thanks to all the hospitable folks who provided advice and insights during our treks in the desert. Please know that you are not forgotten.

Thanks to you all!

Map Legend

Boundaries

National wilderness/preserve boundary

National park boundary

State park boundary

County park boundary

State boundary

Transportation

Interstate

U.S. highway

State highway

Primary road

Other road

Unpaved road

Unimproved road

Featured unimproved road

Featured trail

Optional trail

Other trail

Railroad

Power line

Hydrology

Intermittent stream

Spring

Fall

Lake

Dry lake

Lava bed

Sand/wash

Physiography

×   Spot elevation

)(Pass

▲   Peak

∩   Cave

Cliff

Symbols

Trailhead

Trail start

Trail locator

Trail turnaround

Parking

Restroom/toilet

Campground

Backcountry campground

Lodging

Visitor center

Ranger station

Telephone

Picnic area

Town

Overlook

Point of interest

Mine/prospect

Gate

Bridge

Airport/landing strip

Introduction

The California desert covers the southeastern quarter of our most populous and most ecologically diverse state. Incredibly, three of the four desert subregions that make up most of the arid southwest corner of North America are found within the California desert. These subregions—the Colorado (called the Sonoran in Mexico), Mojave, and Great Basin Deserts—differ by climate and distinct plant and animal communities.

The geographer's definition of a desert as a place with less than 10 inches average annual rainfall says little about what a desert really is. Deserts are regions of irregular and minimal rainfall, so much so that for most of the time, scarcity of water is limiting to life. Averages mean nothing in a desert region that may go one or two years without *any* rain only to receive up to three times the annual average the following year.

In the desert, evaporation far exceeds precipitation. Temperatures swing widely between night and day. This is because low humidity and intense sun heat up the ground during the day, but almost all the heat dissipates at night. Daily temperature changes of 50 degrees or more are common—which can be hazardous to unprepared hikers caught out after dark.

Sparse rainfall means sparse vegetation, which in turn means naked geological features. Most of the California desert is crisscrossed with mountain ranges, imparting an exposed, rough-hewn, scenic character to the landscape. Rather than having been uplifted, the mountains were largely formed by an east-west collision of the earth's tectonic plates, producing a north-south orientation of the ranges. Some would call the result stark, but all would agree that these signatures on the land are dramatic and, at times, overpowering. This very starkness tends to exaggerate the drama of space, color, relief, and sheer ruggedness.

Despite sparse plant cover, the number of individual plant species in the California desert is amazing. At least 1,000 species are spread among 103 vascular plant families. Equally amazing is the diversity of bird life and other wildlife on this deceptively barren land. Many of these birds and animals are active only at night, or are most likely seen during the hotter months at or near watering holes. Hundreds of bird species and more than sixty kinds of reptiles and amphibians fly, nest, crawl, and slither in habitat niches to which they have adapted. Desert bighorn sheep and the rare mountain lion are at the top of the charismatic mega-fauna list, but at least sixty other species of mammals make the desert their home—from kit foxes on the valley floors to squirrels on the highest mountain crests. The best way to observe these desert denizens is on foot, far from the madding crowd, in the peace and solitude of desert wilderness.

Much of Death Valley National Park is on the southwestern edge of the vast Great Basin desert region, which also encompasses most of Nevada, much of Utah, and portions of Oregon, Idaho, and Wyoming. This is high, cold desert, largely above

4,000 feet, with snow and freezing temperatures during winter. The Great Basin is distinguished by sunken interior drainage basins bounded by hundreds of mountain ranges, created by shifting along fault lines. Rubber rabbitbrush, blackbrush, and big sagebrush characterize the plant cover.

Death Valley is included within the Colorado and Mojave Desert Biosphere Reserve, which was internationally designated in 1984. There are more than 265 biosphere reserves worldwide that protect lands within each of the earth's biogeographic regions. The park is within the core of the biosphere reserve, where human impact is kept to a minimum. The core is surrounded by a multiple-use area where sustainable development is the guiding principle. In Death Valley the "human connection" of the reserve is represented by members of the Timbisha Shoshone Indian tribe who live within the park.

Death Valley National Park receives many international visitors who are drawn to the desert because there is no desert in their homeland. Many come during the peak of summer to experience the desert at its hottest. Regardless of whether the visitor is from Europe, a nearby California town, or someplace across the nation, the endlessly varied desert offers something for everyone. Unlike snowbound northern regions, the California desert is a year-round hiker's paradise. There is no better place in which to actually see the raw, exposed forces of land-shaping geology at work. Those interested in history and paleoarchaeology will have a field day. And the list goes on. This book is designed to enhance the enjoyment of all who wish to sample the richness of Death Valley National Park on their own terms. Travel is best done on foot, with distance and destination being far less important than the experience of getting there.

The Meaning and Value of Wilderness

Visitors to Death Valley and other desert wildlands should appreciate the meaning and values of wilderness, if for no other reason than to better enjoy their visits with less impact on the wildland values that attracted them in the first place. Nearly 14 percent of California (almost fourteen million acres) is designated federal wilderness, making the Golden State the premier wilderness state in the continental United States. The California Desert Protection Act of 1994 doubled the wilderness acreage in the state and tripled the amount of wilderness under National Park Service jurisdiction, increasing from two million to six million acres.

Those who know and love wild country have their own personal definition of wilderness, heartfelt and often unexpressed, which varies with each person. But since Congress reserved to itself the exclusive power to designate wilderness in the monumental Wilderness Act of 1964, it is important that we also understand the *legal* meaning of "wilderness."

The most fundamental purpose of the Wilderness Act is to provide an *enduring* resource of wilderness for this and future generations so that a growing, increasingly mechanized human population does not occupy and modify every last wild niche. Just as important as preserving the land is the preservation of natural processes, such as naturally ignited fire, erosion, landslides, and other forces that shape the land. Before 1964 the uncertain whim of administrative fiat was all that protected wilderness. During the 1930s the "commanding general" of the wilderness battle, Wilderness Society cofounder Bob Marshall, described wilderness as a "snowbank melting on a hot June day." In the desert the analogy might be closer to a sand dune shrinking on a windy day.

The act defines wilderness as undeveloped federal lands "where the earth and its community of life are untrammeled by man, where man is a visitor who does not remain." In old English the word "trammel" means a net, so "untrammeled" conveys the idea of land that is unnetted or uncontrolled by humans. Congress recognized that no land is completely free of human influence, going on to say that wilderness must "generally appear to have been affected primarily by the forces of nature, with the imprint of man's work substantially unnoticeable." Further, a "wilderness" must have outstanding opportunities for solitude or primitive and unconfined recreation, and be at least 5,000 acres in size or large enough to preserve and use in an unimpaired condition. Also, wilderness may contain ecological, geological, or other features of scientific, educational, scenic, or historical value. Death Valley National Park meets and easily exceeds these legal requirements. Any lingering doubts are removed by the distant music of a coyote beneath a star-studded desert sky, or by the soothing rhythm of an oasis waterfall in a remote canyon.

In general, wilderness designation protects the land from development such as roads, buildings, motorized vehicles, and equipment, and from commercial uses except preexisting livestock grazing, outfitting, and the development of mining claims and leases validated before the 1984 cutoff date in the federal Wilderness Act. The act set up the National Wilderness System and empowered three federal agencies to administer wilderness: the Forest Service, the Fish and Wildlife Service, and the National Park Service. The Bureau of Land Management was added to the list with passage of the 1976 Federal Land Policy and Management Act. These agencies can and do make wilderness recommendations, as any citizen can, but only Congress can set aside wilderness on federal lands. This is where politics enters in, epitomizing the kind of grassroots democracy that eventually brought about passage of the landmark California Desert Protection Act. The formula for wilderness conservationists has been and continues to be "endless pressure endlessly applied."

But once designated, the unending job of wilderness stewardship is just beginning. The managing agencies have a special responsibility to administer wilderness in "such manner as will leave them (wilderness areas) unimpaired for future use and enjoyment *as wilderness.*" Unimpairment of wilderness over time can only be achieved through partnership between concerned citizens and the agencies.

Wilderness is the only truly biocentric use of land. It is off-limits to intensive human uses with an objective of preserving the diversity of nonhuman life, which is richly endowed in the California desert. As such, its preservation is our society's highest act of humility. This is where we deliberately slow down our impulse to drill the last barrel of oil, mine the last vein of ore, or build a parking lot on top of the last wild peak. The desert wilderness explorer can take genuine pride in reaching a remote summit under his or her power, traversing a narrow serpentine canyon, or walking across the uncluttered expanse of a vast desert basin. Hiking boots and self-reliance replace motorized equipment and push-button convenience, allowing us to find something in ourselves we feared lost.

Have Fun and Be Safe

Wandering in the desert has a reputation of being a dangerous activity, thanks to both the Bible and Hollywood. Usually depicted as a wasteland, the desert evokes fear. With proper planning, however, desert hiking is not hazardous. In fact, it is fun and exciting and is quite safe.

An enjoyable desert outing requires preparation. Beginning with this book, along with the maps suggested in the hike write-ups, you need to be equipped with adequate knowledge about your hiking area. Carry good maps and a compass, and know how to use them.

Calculating the time required for a hike in the desert defies any formula. Terrain is often rough; extensive detours around boulders, dry falls, and drop-offs mean longer trips. Straight-line distance is an illusion. Sun, heat, and wind likewise all conspire to slow down even the speediest hiker. Therefore, distances are not what they appear in the desert. Five desert miles may take longer than 10 woodland miles. Plan your excursion conservatively, and always carry emergency items in your pack (see appendix B).

While you consult the equipment list (appendix B), note that water ranks the highest. Carrying the water is not enough—take the time to stop and drink it. This is another reason desert hikes take longer. Frequent water breaks are mandatory. It's best to return from your hike with empty water bottles. You can cut down on loss of bodily moisture by hiking with your mouth closed and breathing through your nose; reduce thirst also by avoiding sweets and alcohol.

Driving to and from the trailhead is statistically far more dangerous than hiking in the desert backcountry. But being far from the nearest 911 service requires knowledge about possible hazards and proper precautions to avoid them. It is not an oxymoron to have fun and to be safe. Quite to the contrary: If you're not safe, you won't have fun. At the risk of creating excessive paranoia, here are the treacherous twelve:

Dehydration

It cannot be overemphasized that plenty of water is necessary for desert hiking. Carry one gallon per person per day in unbreakable plastic screw-top containers. And pause often to drink it. Carry water in your car as well so you'll have water to return to. As a general rule, plain water is a better thirst-quencher than any of the colored fluids on the market, which usually generate greater thirst. It is very important to maintain proper electrolyte balance by eating small quantities of nutritional foods throughout the day, even if you feel you don't have an appetite.

Changeable Weather

The desert is well known for sudden changes in the weather. The temperature can change 50 degrees in less than an hour. Prepare yourself with extra food and clothing, rain/wind gear, and a flashlight. When leaving on a trip, let someone know your exact route, especially if traveling solo, and your estimated time of return; don't forget to let them know when you get back. Register your route at the closest park office or backcountry board, especially for longer hikes that involve cross-country travel.

Hypothermia/Hyperthermia

Abrupt chilling is as much a danger in the desert as heat stroke. Storms and/or nightfall can cause desert temperatures to plunge. Wear layers of clothes, adding or subtracting depending on conditions, to avoid overheating or chilling. At the other extreme, you need to protect yourself from sun and wind with proper clothing. The broad-brimmed hat is mandatory equipment for the desert traveler. Even in the cool days of winter, a delightful time in the desert, the sun's rays are intense.

Vegetation

You quickly will learn not to come in contact with certain desert vegetation. Catclaw, Spanish bayonet, and cacti are just a few of the botanical hazards that will get your attention if you become complacent. Carry tweezers to extract cactus spines. Wear long pants if traveling off-trail or in a brushy area. Many folks carry a hair comb to assist with removal of cholla balls.

Rattlesnakes, Scorpions, Tarantulas

These desert "creepy crawlies" are easily terrified by unexpected human visitors, and they react predictably to being frightened. Do not sit or put your hands in dark places you can't see, especially during the warmer "snake season" months. Carry and know how to use your snakebite-venom-extractor kit for emergencies when help is far away. In the event of a snakebite, seek medical assistance as quickly as possible. Keep tents zipped and always shake out boots, packs, and clothes before putting them on.

Mountain Lions

The California desert is mountain-lion country. Avoid hiking at night, when lions are often hunting. Instruct your children on appropriate behavior when confronted with a lion. Do not run. Keep children in sight while hiking; stay close to them in areas where lions might hide.

Mine Hazards

The California desert contains thousands of deserted mines. All of them should be considered hazardous. Stay away from all mines and mine structures. The vast majority of these mines have not been secured or even posted. Keep an eye on young or adventuresome members of your group.

Hanta Virus

In addition to the mines, there are often deserted buildings around the mine sites. Hanta virus is a deadly disease carried by deer mice in the Southwest. Any enclosed area increases the chances of breathing the airborne particles that carry this life-threatening virus. As a precaution, do not enter deserted buildings.

Flash Floods

Desert washes and canyons can become traps for unwary visitors when rainstorms hit the desert. Keep a watchful eye on the sky. Never camp in flash-flood areas. Check at a ranger station on regional weather conditions before embarking on your backcountry expedition. A storm anywhere upstream in a drainage can result in a sudden torrent in a lower canyon. Do not cross a flooded wash. Both the depth and the current can be deceiving; wait for the flood to recede, which usually does not take long.

Lightning

Be aware of lightning, especially during summer storms. Stay off ridges and peaks. Shallow overhangs and gullies should also be avoided because electrical current often moves at ground level near a lightning strike.

Unstable Rocky Slopes

Desert canyons and mountainsides often consist of crumbly or fragmented rock. Mountain sheep are better adapted to this terrain than us bipeds. Use caution when climbing; the downward journey is usually the more hazardous. Smooth rock faces such as in slickrock canyons are equally dangerous, especially when you've got sand on the soles of your boots. On those rare occasions when they are wet, the rocks are slicker than ice.

Giardia

Any surface water, with the possible exception of springs where they flow out of the ground, is apt to contain *Giardia lamblia,* a microorganism that causes severe diarrhea. Boil water for at least five minutes or use a filter system. Iodine drops are not effective in killing this pesky parasite.

Zero-Impact Desert Etiquette

The desert environment is fragile; damage lasts for decades—even centuries. Desert courtesy requires us to leave no evidence that we were ever there. This ethic means no grafitti or defoliation at one end of the spectrum, and no unnecessary footprints on delicate vegetation on the other. Here are seven general guidelines for desert wilderness behavior:

Avoid making new trails. If hiking cross-country, stay on one set of footprints when traveling in a group. Try to make your route invisible. Desert vegetation grows very slowly. Its destruction leads to wind and water erosion and irreparable harm to the desert. Darker crusty soil that crumbles easily indicates cryptogamic soils, which are a living blend of tightly bonded mosses, lichens, and bacteria. This dark crust prevents wind and water erosion and protects seeds that fall into the soil. Walking can destroy this fragile layer. Take special care to avoid stepping on cryptogamic soil.

Keep noise down. Desert wilderness means quiet and solitude, for the animal life as well as other human visitors.

Leave your pets at home. Check with park authorities before including your dog in the group. Better yet, share other experiences with your best friend, not the desert.

Pack it in/pack it out. This is more true in the desert than anywhere else. Desert winds spread debris, and desert air preserves it. Always carry a trash bag, both for your trash and for any that you encounter. If you must smoke, pick up your butts and bag them. Bag and carry out toilet paper (it doesn't deteriorate in the desert) and feminine hygiene products.

Never camp near water. Most desert animals are nocturnal, and most, like the bighorn sheep, are exceptionally shy. The presence of humans is very disturbing, so camping near their water source means they will go without water. Camp in already-used sites if possible to reduce further damage. If none is available, camp on ground that is already bare. And use a camp stove. Ground fires are forbidden in most desert parks; gathering wood is also not permitted. Leave your campsite as you found it. Better yet, improve it by picking up litter, cleaning out fire rings, or scattering ashes of any inconsiderate predecessors. Remember that artifacts fifty years old or older are protected by federal law, and must not be moved or removed.

Treat human waste properly. Bury human waste 4 inches deep and at least 200 feet from water and trails. Pack out toilet paper and feminine hygiene products; they do not decompose in the arid desert. Do not burn toilet paper; many wildfires have been started this way.

Respect wildlife. Living in the desert is hard enough without being harassed by human intruders. Remember this is the only home these animals have. They treasure their privacy. Be respectful and use binoculars for long-distance viewing. *Especially important:* Do not molest the rare desert water sources by playing or bathing in them.

Beyond these guidelines, refer to the regulations of Death Valley National Park for specific rules governing backcountry usage. Enjoy the beauty and solitude of the desert, and leave it for others to enjoy.

How to Use This Book

This guide is *the* source book for those who wish to experience on foot the very best hikes and backcountry trips Death Valley National Park has to offer. Hikers are given many choices from which they can pick and choose, depending on their wishes and abilities.

The maps in this book that depict a detailed close-up of an area use elevation tints, called hypsometry, to portray relief. Each gray tone represents a range of equal elevation, as shown in the scale key with the map. These maps will give you a good idea of elevation gain and loss. The darker tones are lower elevations and the lighter grays are higher elevations. The lighter the tone, the higher the elevation. Narrow bands of different gray tones spaced closely together indicate steep terrain, whereas wider bands indicate areas of more gradual slope.

Maps that show larger geographic areas use shaded, or shadow, relief. Shadow relief does not represent elevation; it demonstrates slope or relative steepness. This gives an almost 3-D perspective of the physiography of a region and will help you see where ranges and valleys are.

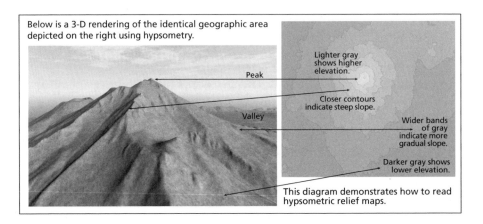

Below is a 3-D rendering of the identical geographic area depicted on the right using hypsometry.

Peak

Valley

Lighter gray shows higher elevation.

Closer contours indicate steep slope.

Wider bands of gray indicate more gradual slope.

Darker gray shows lower elevation.

This diagram demonstrates how to read hypsometric relief maps.

Begin by referring to the hike locator map on page 12, along with the "Hikes at a Glance" matrix for a quick overview of all of the hikes presented for the park. After making your selections, turn to the specific hike descriptions for added detail. Each hike is numbered and named and begins with a general description. This overview briefly describes the type of hike and highlights the destination and key features.

The "start" is the approximate road distance from a nearby town or park visitor center to the trailhead. The idea is to give you a mental picture of where the hike is in relation to your prospective travels.

Hike "distance" is given in total miles for the described route. The mileage is in one direction for a loop, in which you return to the place where you started without retracing your steps, or for a one-way hike, in which you begin at one trailhead and end at another, requiring two vehicles, a shuttle bus, or another driver to pick you up or deposit you at either end. Round-trip mileage is provided for an out-and-back hike, in which you return to the trailhead the same way you came. A lollipop loop combines a stretch of out-and-back with a loop at one end. Mileages were calculated in the field and double-checked as accurately as possible with the most detailed topographic maps.

"Approximate hiking time" provides a best guess as to how long it will take the average hiker to complete the route. Always add more time for further exploration or for contemplation.

The "difficulty" rating is necessarily subjective, but it is based on the authors' extensive backcountry experience with folks of all ages and abilities. Easy hikes present no difficulty to hikers of all abilities. Moderate hikes are challenging to inexperienced hikers and might tax even experienced hikers. Strenuous hikes are extremely difficult and challenging, even for the most-seasoned hikers. Distance, elevation gain and loss, trail condition, and terrain were considered in assigning the difficulty rating. There are, of course, many variables. The easiest hike can be sheer torture if you run out of water in extreme heat—a definite no-no.

"Trail surfaces" are evaluated based on well-defined trail standards. Dirt trails have no obstructions and are easy to follow. Rocky trails may be partially blocked by slides, rocks, or debris but are generally obvious and easy to find. Primitive trails are faint, rough, and rocky and may have disappeared completely in places. In the desert some of the best hiking takes place on old four-wheel-drive mining roads that are now closed to vehicular use because of wilderness designation or to protect key values, such as wildlife watering holes. Many of the desert hikes are off-trail in washes, canyons, ridges, and fans. "Use trails" may form a segment of the route. A use trail is simply an informal, unconstructed path created solely by the passage of hikers.

The best "season" is based largely on the moderate-temperature months for the particular hike and is greatly influenced by elevation. Additional consideration is given to seasonal road access at higher altitudes. The range of months given is not necessarily the best time for wildflowers, which is highly localized and dependent on elevation and rainfall. Nor is it necessarily the best time to view wildlife, which may be during the driest and hottest summer months near water sources.

The maps listed are the best available for route-finding and land navigation: the relevant 7.5-minute topographic map (1:24,000 scale or 2.6 inches = 1 mile) with a 40-foot contour interval. These U.S. Geological Survey maps can usually be purchased at the park visitor centers. They can also be purchased for $6.00 each (price as of this writing) directly from Map Distribution, USGS Map Sales, Box 25286, Federal Center, Building 810, Denver, CO 80225; by calling (800) ASK–USGS; or online at www.usgs.gov/pubprod/. See appendix C for a listing of other useful smaller-scale maps.

For more information on the hike, the best available "trail contact" for the park management agency is listed. See appendix D for a complete listing of all agency addresses and phone numbers.

"Finding the trailhead" includes detailed up-to-date driving instructions to the trailhead or jumping-off point for each hike. For most hikes, there is no formal trailhead but rather a starting point where you can park. To follow these instructions, start with the beginning reference point, which might be the park visitor center, a nearby town, or an important road junction. Pay close attention to mileage and landmark instructions. American Automobile Association (AAA) map mileages are used when available, but in many instances we had to rely on our car odometer, which may vary slightly from other car odometers.

The text following the driving directions is a narrative of the actual route with general directions and key features noted. In some cases interpretation of the natural and cultural history of the hike and its surroundings is included. The idea is to provide accurate route-finding instructions, with enough supporting information to enhance your enjoyment of the hike without diminishing your sense of discovery— a fine line indeed. Some of these descriptions are augmented with photographs that preview a representative segment of the hike.

The trail itinerary, "Miles and Directions," provides detailed mile-by-mile instructions while noting landmarks, trail junctions, canyon entrances, dry falls, peaks, and historic sites along the way.

And last, please don't allow our value-laden list of "favorite hikes" (appendix A) to discourage you from completing any of the other hikes. They're all worth doing!

Death Valley National Park

eath Valley's intimidating name is said to have originated in 1849 when an anonymous member of the forty-niners, after nearly dying while seeking a shortcut to the newly discovered California goldfields, turned around at the final view and exclaimed, "Good-bye, Death Valley!" Now it's our turn to say hello to one of the world's most imposing and contrasting landscapes. The extremes of Death Valley, from soaring snowcapped peaks to North America's hottest, driest, and lowest desert, command respect and entice discovery.

In 1933 President Herbert Hoover proclaimed Death Valley a national monument, a status less protective than that of national park because of mining conflicts. The monument was expanded in 1937 when President Franklin Roosevelt added the 300,000-acre Nevada triangle. In 1952 President Truman added forty acres of Devil's Hole in Nevada to protect a rare variety of desert pupfish. With mining a major issue in Death Valley, the 1976 Mining in Parks Act is of special significance. This law began phasing out mining in the monument by closing Death Valley to the filing of new claims. The number of old claims has since decreased from 50,000 to fewer than 150, with only one active mine remaining.

The status of the monument was further elevated in 1984 when the United Nations recognized Death Valley as part of the Mojave and Colorado International Biosphere Reserve. Finally, on October 31, 1994, Death Valley received long overdue national park classification when President Bill Clinton signed the California Desert Protection Act into law. The 2-million-acre national monument became a more than 3.3-million-acre national park, with 95 percent of the park designated wilderness. In so doing, Death Valley became the nation's largest national park outside Alaska.

A Long and Complex Geologic Past

The land of extremes that is Death Valley is best dramatized when afternoon shadows from 11,049-foot Telescope Peak are cast across the Badwater Basin, 282 feet below sea level. Combine this amazing vertical relief with recent volcanic craters,

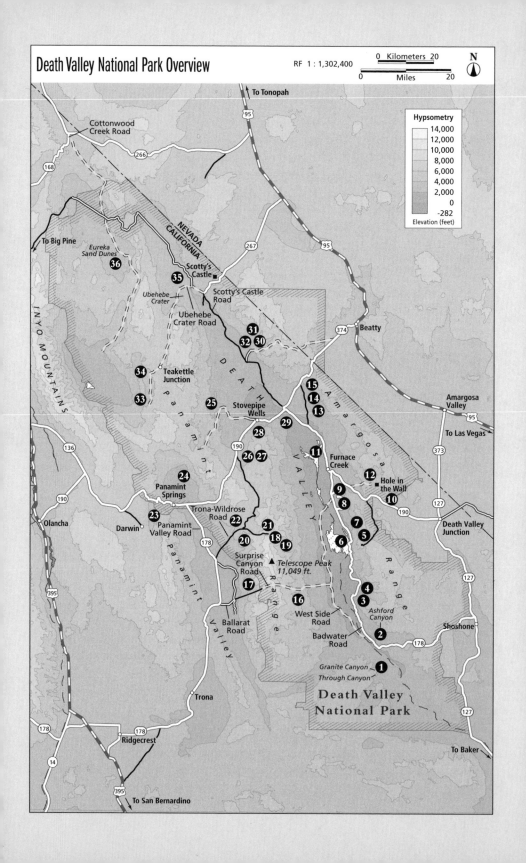

Death Valley National Park Overview

RF 1 : 1,302,400

0 ___ Kilometers ___ 20

0 ___ Miles ___ 20

N

Hypsometry

14,000
12,000
10,000
8,000
6,000
4,000
2,000
0
-282
Elevation (feet)

To Tonopah

95

Cottonwood
Creek Road

266

168

NEVADA
CALIFORNIA

To Big Pine

Eureka
Sand Dunes

36

35

Scotty's
Castle

267

95

Beatty

374

Scotty's Castle
Road

Ubehebe
Crater

Ubehebe
Crater Road

31
32 **30**

34 Teakettle
Junction

33

INYO MOUNTAINS

DEATH

Panamint

25

Stovepipe
Wells

29

28

15
14
13

Amargosa

Amargosa
Valley

95

To Las Vegas

373

136

190

26 **27**

11

Furnace
Creek

12

Hole in
the Wall

127

24

Panamint
Springs

Trona-Wildrose
Road

23

22

9
8

10

190

7
5

Death Valley
Junction

Olancha

190

Darwin

Panamint
Valley Road

178

21
20 **18**
19

6

Surprise
Canyon
Road

▲ Telescope Peak
11,049 ft.

395

17

16

West Side
Road

4
3

Ashford
Canyon

Shoshone

2

127

Ballarat
Road

Badwater
Road

VALLEY

Range

Panamint

Range

Valley

Trona

Granite Canyon

Through Canyon

1

**Death Valley
National Park**

127

178

Ridgecrest

178

To Baker

14

395

To San Bernardino

towering sand dunes, and flood-scoured canyons and you begin to appreciate a long and complicated geologic history.

Death Valley is at the western and youngest edge of the Basin and Range Province (the Great Basin). As such, its relatively youthful topography is extreme, with mountains still growing and basins still sinking. The oldest rocks date back 1.8 billion years but have been too severely changed to be reliably interpreted for geologic history.

Rocks a mere half billion years old are more predictable. The Funeral and Panamint Mountains are made up of these weathered limestones and sandstones. The rocks point to a warm, shallow sea from around 570 million to 250 million years ago. The sea left layers of sediment and a myriad of marine fossils. Between 1933 and 1994 researchers discovered 500 species of fossil plants and animals within the monument. Now that the boundaries have been expanded by 50 percent, the new park may prove to be the most fossil-rich national park in the United States and perhaps in the world.

Death Valley is next to the boundary of two interconnected plates in the earth's crust. When the plates moved slowly in relation to each other, compression folded and fractured the brittle crust. This caused the land surface to push up and the sea to gradually recede west. Most of this faulting took place from 250 million to 70 million years ago. Active mountain building then alternated with inactive periods of mountain-reducing erosion.

Volcanic activity prevailed from seventy million to three million years ago. Mountain building stretched and weakened the earth's crust, forming weak spots through which molten material could erupt. This volcanic activity moved westward from Nevada, producing a chain of volcanoes east of the park from Furnace Creek southeast to Shoshone. Eruptions of cinder and ash account for the flamboyant colors of borate mineral deposits at Artist's Palette.

Around three million years ago, the floor of Death Valley began to form. Compression was replaced by a pulling apart of the earth's crust, causing large blocks of land to slowly slide past one another along faults. These extensional forces formed parallel north-south trending valleys and mountain ranges. The salt flats of Badwater Basin and the Panamint Range make up one block that is rotating to the east. The valley floor, known as a half-graben, continues to slip down along the fault at the foot of the Black Mountains. This dropping is evident in recently exposed fault scarps near Badwater. Meanwhile, erosion continues with flash floods carrying rocks, sand, and gravel from surrounding hillsides to alluvial fans that spread like gigantic funnels from every canyon mouth. More than 9,000 feet of sediments and salts lie beneath the half-graben floor at Badwater.

Climate has also been a major force in these ongoing changes. During the last major continental ice age, the bottom of Death Valley was covered by a system of huge lakes. As the climate warmed, the lakes disappeared—about 10,000 years ago.

Death Valley serves as a backdrop for the remains of the miner's cabin at Keane Wonder Spring.

A much smaller lake system formed 2,000 years ago during a cold period. This water then evaporated, leaving behind today's salt deposits.

The Ubehebe Craters in the northern end of the park tell the tale of recent volcanic activity of several thousand years ago. The craters were formed by violent steam explosions caused when molten material mixed with groundwater. Erosion, earthquakes, and subsidence continue to reshape the surface of one of North America's most dramatic and ever-changing landscapes.

A Tapestry of Life: Don't Let the Name Fool You

More than 1,000 plant species thrive in the incredibly wide range of elevations and habitats found within the park—from dry alkali flats below sea level to the subalpine crests of the highest Panamint summits. These species include nineteen endemics found *only* within the boundaries of the park, such as telescope bedstraw, Panamint monkey flower, and Eureka Dunes evening primrose. Another twenty-three species have the majority of their range within the park, such as magnificent lupine and

Death Valley sage. No fewer than thirteen species of cactus grow within the park. Ironically, this driest of deserts is home to more species of marsh grass than cactus.

Spring wildflowers are a pageant worth waiting for. The white of desert-star, red of Indian paintbrush, pink of desert five-spot, yellow of desert gold, and blue of Arizona lupine are what dreams are made of. But as with everything, there are good years and bad years. A spectacular year for the showy plants of these desert annuals depends on well-spaced rainfall throughout winter and early spring, enough warming sun, and few drying winds. The premier blooming periods in the park are usually late February to mid-April in the lower elevations of valley floors and alluvial fans, early April to early May for midslopes up to 4,000 feet, and late April to early June above 4,000 feet in the Panamints and other mountain ranges.

Death Valley is home to at least fifty-one species of mammals, thirty-six species of reptiles, five species of amphibians, and six species of fishes. Some of the animals, such as desert bighorn sheep, live near springs in inaccessible mountains and canyons. The nocturnal kit fox is common in most of Death Valley. Coyotes may be seen from the salt flats up to the highest mountain plateaus. Some species have been introduced, such as the burro was in the 1880s. The reptile list includes the threatened desert tortoise and the mostly nocturnal Mojave sidewinder rattlesnake. Five species of desert pupfish live in the park, four of which are endemic to Death Valley. These endemics are the Saratoga pupfish, Salt Creek pupfish, threatened Cottonball Marsh pupfish, and the endangered Devil's Hole pupfish. These tiny members of the killfish family vary from 1 to 2.5 inches long. They lived in ancient freshwater lakes during the last ice age. As the climate became drier, the pupfish became isolated in widely separated warm springs and creeks, gradually adapting to higher temperatures and increased salinity.

Human History

Death Valley has been the site of at least four Native American cultures, beginning about 10,000 years ago with a group of hunter-gatherers known as "the Nevares Spring people." Game was abundant during this wetter period. As the climate became drier, they were replaced by the Mesquite Flat people about 4,000 years later. Then the Saratoga Spring people arrived about 2,000 years ago when the hot, dry desert was similar to today's conditions. These people were skilled hunters who created large, intricate stone patterns in the valley. Nomadic desert Shoshone moved into the valley about 1,000 years ago. Like many people today, they camped near water sources in the valley during winter, then headed up into the cooler mountains during summer to escape searing heat.

The first non-native people to enter the valley were two groups of emigrants on their way to the California goldfields in 1849. From the 1880s to early 1900s, mining was sporadic in the region. Lack of suitable transportation limited mining to only the highest-grade ore. Perhaps the best-known but shortest-lived mine was the Harmony

Borax Works, active from 1883 to 1888. It was most famous for its twenty-mule wagons and the *Death Valley Days* radio and television programs. W. T. Coleman built the wagons that hauled the processed mineral 165 miles across the desert to the railroad at Mojave. Gold and silver mining picked up in the early 1900s with such large-scale ventures as the Keane Wonder Mine, but then came the Panic of 1907. Profitable large-scale hardrock mining in Death Valley ended around 1915. During World War II talc was mined here until markets made mining unprofitable. In 1989 these talc-mining claims were bought by the Conservation Foundation and donated to the National Park Service in 1992.

Weather

This land of extremes doesn't end with topography, vertical relief, and a Noah's ark of wildlife. Recorded temperatures range from a sizzling 134 degrees to a freezing low of 15 degrees. The valley experiences an average annual temperature of 76 pleasant degrees—somewhat deceiving given the summer averages at well above 100 degrees. Temperatures will be 3 to 5 degrees cooler along with increased precipitation for every 1,000-foot vertical increase in elevation. One balmy July day in 1972, with the air temperature at 128 degrees, a ground temperature of 201 degrees was measured at Furnace Creek. With no protective shade, any attempt to hike the salt flats in these conditions could be a terminal experience. For hiking comfort, November to April is hard to beat. Average highs are in the 60- to 90-degree range on the valley floor, cooling considerably at higher elevations. The loftiest mountaintops are often snow-covered from November to May.

Precipitation figures can be misleading, as an annual average of less than 2 inches of rain falls in Death Valley. The mountain ranges can catch torrential winter downpours, causing flash flooding, road closures, and trail washouts. To check on current road and trail conditions, consult the Death Valley Web site (www.nps.gov/deva) before heading to the desert.

Rules to Enjoy the Park

At this time overnight backcountry hikers and campers are not required to obtain a permit, which is unusual for a "big name" national park. This may change, so always check the park's Web site or the visitor center for the latest regulations. However, filling out a backcountry registration form is recommended for backpackers. These forms are available at the Furnace Creek Visitor Center or at any ranger station.

Limited open-desert car camping is allowed at Death Valley, a sprawling park with more than three million acres of wilderness and 600-plus miles of dirt roads. The basic rule is that backcountry camping is permitted 2 miles beyond any paved

◀ *Dante's View provides a spectacular panorama of Badwater 6,000 feet below, with the snow-capped 11,049-foot Telescope Peak in the distance.*

road, day-use-only area, or developed area. Car campers must use preexisting campsites and park next to the roadway to reduce impact and to avoid violating the wilderness boundary, which, in most cases, closely parallels the road. A high-clearance vehicle is usually needed to travel 2 or more miles from pavement on a dirt road that is open for camping. Camping is not allowed on day-use-only roads, including the Titus Canyon Road, West Side Road, Wildrose Road, and Racetrack Road from Teakettle Junction to Homestake Dry Camp. Camping is also prohibited at three historic mining areas, including the Ubehebe Lead Mine. Actually, the safe thing to do is to avoid camping at any mining area. Backcountry camping is not allowed on the valley floor from 2 miles north of Stovepipe Wells south to Ashford Mill.

Overnight group size is limited to fifteen people and no more than six vehicles. Campsites in the backcountry must be at least 200 yards from any water source to avoid disturbing wildlife in these fragile and limited sites. In view of the recent park and wilderness designations at Death Valley, it is important to obtain a copy of the latest backcountry regulations at the Furnace Creek Visitor Center or nearest ranger station.

Off-road vehicle use is prohibited, not only because the land away from roads is wilderness and closed to motorized use, but also because the desert is fragile and painfully slow to recover from damage. Bicycles are permitted on all paved and open dirt roads but are not allowed on trails, off roads, or in park wilderness. Campfires are only allowed in fire pits at developed campgrounds. If you want a fire, bring wood in from outside; gathering the scarce wood here is unlawful. Remember that the park is a museum of undisturbed nature, so removal of any rocks, wood, plants, animals, or historic artifacts is prohibited.

No matter how pitiful the begging coyote may appear, do not feed wildlife. To do so causes them to depend on unnatural food sources, which is tantamount to a death sentence. Speaking of animals, leave your pets at home if at all possible. They must be restrained at all times and are not allowed off roads, on trails, or in park wilderness. Of course, any type of weapon is strictly prohibited in the park.

Campgrounds, Services, Fees

Nine developed National Park Service campgrounds with more than 1,500 sites are well distributed in the central to north-central region of the park. Four of these are free, one of which, Wildrose, is open year-round, weather permitting. The Wildrose Campground is reached by way of the rough Wildrose Canyon Road. The other three higher-elevation campgrounds, Emigrant, Thorndike, and Mahogany Flat, are open spring to fall depending on weather conditions. Of the five fee campgrounds, Furnace Creek and Mesquite Spring are open all year. Texas Spring, Sunset, and Stovepipe Wells are at or below sea level and are open October to April.

The main visitor center and Death Valley Natural History Association (DVNHA) is located at Furnace Creek, with other visitor centers at Beatty, Nevada, and Scotty's Castle. Scotty's Castle Visitor Center and Museum is open every day all year from 8:30 A.M. to 5:00 P.M. The main visitor center and museum at Furnace Creek is open from 8:00 A.M. to 5:00 P.M. These hours are subject to change, so check at the park upon your arrival. The National Park Service has prepared an excellent series of free handouts on such topics as geology, mining history, plants, wildflowers, wildlife, special points of interest, and more. During the high season of November through April, rangers and naturalists present evening talks and guided nature walks.

The two park entrance stations are located at Furnace Creek and Grapevine, which is 3.5 miles from Scotty's Castle. The entrance fee is $20 per vehicle and is good for seven days. A Death Valley National Park annual pass is also available for $40. A $50 Golden Eagle Pass provides unlimited admission to the entire National Park System nationwide and is good for one year. U.S. citizens sixty-two and older can purchased a one-time Golden Age Pass for $10, which allows unlimited entry to all National Park System areas. Golden Age Pass holders also receive a 50 percent discount on campground fees.

Food, supplies, and gas can be purchased at Furnace Creek Ranch and Stovepipe Wells. Fuel can also be bought at Scotty's Castle. Distances in the sprawling park are vast, so be sure to travel with plenty of gas, water, food, and other necessary supplies.

The few trails in the park that are formally maintained are described in some of the recommended hikes that follow. Use trails in drainages may largely disappear after a flash flood. Many of the trailless routes follow natural corridors, such as deep canyons. In the desert, hiking use is generally light with vast distances between trailheads, which, in turn, lead to routes without directional signs. Lack of hiker conveniences found in other, more heavily visited parks and wilderness is more than made up for by solitude, and by the spirit of adventure that awaits those willing to explore this magnificent park on foot.

How to Get There

Primary road access to the park from the south is via California Highway 127 from Interstate 15 at Baker. California Highway 178 leads west into the park from CA 127 near Shoshone. California Highway 190 heads west into the park from CA 127 at Death Valley Junction. On the west side, CA 178 takes off from U.S. Highway 395 and enters the park by way of Panamint Valley. CA 190 takes off to the east from US 395 at Olancha, entering the park just west of Panamint Springs. The network of roads within the park run the gamut, from all-weather pavement to a series of rocky washboard ruts that can loosen every bolt and try the patience of the most determined motorist. The closest large commercial airport is at Las Vegas, about 135 miles southeast of Furnace Creek.

Death Valley National Park Hikes at a Glance

Hike and Hike Number	Distance	Difficulty*	Features	Page
Ashford Canyon/Mine (2)	3.0 miles	M	mine site	24
Badwater (6)	1.0 mile	E	salt flats	36
Dante's View (5)	1.0 mile	E	vista	33
Darwin Falls (23)	3.0 miles	S	stream, fall, vista	83
Desolation Canyon (8)	5.2 miles	M	canyon/vista	40
Eureka Dunes (36)	3.0 miles	M	sand dunes	125
Fall Canyon (31)	16.0 miles	S	dry fall, canyon	109
Golden Canyon/ Gower Gulch Loop (9)	6.5 miles	M	scenery, geology	43
Grotto Canyon (27)	4.0 miles	E	canyon	98
Harmony Borax Works (11)	1.0 mile	E	historic site, salt flats (option)	48
Hummingbird Spring (20)	3.0 miles	M	historic site, vista	77
Hungry Bill's Ranch/ Johnson Canyon (16)	3.8 miles	S	historic site, vista	62
Keane Wonder Mine (13)	4.0 miles	S	mill and mine site	54
Keane Wonder Spring (14)	2.0 miles	E	spring, mine site	57
Little Bridge Canyon (28)	7.0 miles	S	canyon	100
Marble Canyon (25)	9.6 miles	M	canyon, archaeology	90
Monarch Canyon/Mine (15)	3.0 miles	E	dry fall, mill site	59
Mosaic Canyon (26)	3.6 miles	M	canyon	94
Natural Bridge (7)	2.0 miles	E	geology, canyon	38
Nemo Canyon (22)	3.6 miles	M	canyon	81
Panamint Dunes (24)	9.0 miles	M	sand dunes	86
Pyramid Canyon (10)	4.0 miles	M	canyon, geology	47
Red Wall Canyon (32)	7.0 miles	M	canyon	112
Salt Creek Interpretive Trail (29)	0.5 mile	E	nature trail	103
Sidewinder Canyon (3)	4.6 miles	M	canyon	26
South Fork Hanaupah Canyon (19)	6.0 miles	M	mine site, scenery	74
Surprise Canyon/Panamint City (17)	13.0 miles	S	stream, canyon, mine/townsite	66
Telescope Peak (18)	14.0 miles	S	vista	70
Through-Granite Canyons (1)	15.0 miles	S	remoteness, scenery	21
Titus Canyon Narrows (30)	4.2 miles	E	canyon	106
Klare Spring	12.0 miles	S	canyon, spring	108
Ubehebe/Little Hebe Craters (35)	1.5 miles	E	volcanic craters	122
Ubehebe Lead Mine/ Corridor Canyon (34)	6.0 miles	M	mine site/canyon	119
Ubehebe Peak (33)	6.2 miles	S	vista	115
Upper Hole-in-the-Wall (12)	11.0 miles	S	canyon, geology	50
Wildrose Peak (21)	8.4 miles	S	vista	79
Willow Canyon (4)	5.0 miles	M	canyon	30

*E=easy, M=moderate, S=strenuous

1 Through-Granite Canyons

A long, challenging canyon loop in the wild, lightly visited Owlshead Mountains, these canyons take you to a remote desert range in the southern end of the park.

Start: About 54 miles south of Furnace Creek.
Distance: 15-mile lollipop.
Approximate hiking time: 8 to 10 hours.
Difficulty: Strenuous.
Trail surface: Off-trail sandy washes, gravelly fans, and canyons with short rocky sections.

Seasons: November through March.
USGS topo maps: Confidence Hills East-CA and Confidence Hills West-CA (1:24,000).
Trail contact: Furnace Creek Visitor Center & Museum (see appendix D).

Finding the trailhead: From Ashford Junction on Badwater Road (California Highway 178), 26 miles southwest of Shoshone and 48 miles south of Furnace Creek, drive south on the wide gravel Harry Wade Road. After about 5.9 slow miles, look for a wide parking spot alongside the bermed roadway, which will be next to Confidence Wash and about 1 mile before the Confidence Mill site. Driving Harry Wade Road from the south is not recommended because it is four-wheel drive at best and impassable during flooding.

The Hike

Upon reaching the jumping-off point for this lengthy desert trek, you'll have driven through a section of Death Valley known as "the Narrows." The brown Confidence Hills to the immediate west are an eroded scarp of the southern Death Valley fault. It was once believed that the adventurous Harry Wade family used the road as an escape route from Death Valley in 1850.

From your parking spot, you can see the prominent rounded hill beyond the Confidence Hills that forms the southern gateway to Through Canyon. A higher range of mountains rises beyond. Begin by hiking southwesterly toward the trailing southern edge of the Confidence Hills. Soon you'll cross the broad, gravelly creosote plain of the normally dry Amargosa River. Skirt around the hills to the lower wash of Granite Canyon. Hike up the wide, high-walled wash to the forks of the wash at about 2 miles. Cross the wash and continue to hike southwesterly toward Through Canyon, reaching the mouth at about 4.3 miles. To the immediate south is the prominent rounded hill that you could see from the trailhead. Look back, to the east, for varied views of fans, buttes, and the jagged teeth of volcanic peaks.

Hillsides bordering the wash are a jumble of volcanic rock with granitic bedrock. In the spring you might see flowering buttercups and the tiny blue flowers of chia along with desert holly, smoke trees, creosote and saltbush, to name only a few. You'll follow the trails of feral burros for the next couple of miles, with color-banded shades of red, white, and brown rock overhead. The valley splits about 2.3 miles above the mouth; keep to the right. Another mile brings you to a broad upper

Looking down the upper reaches of Through Canyon.

basin. The main wash curves left to the horizon. Angle to the right (north) for the crossover to Granite Canyon. Continue right as the valley steepens, reaching a saddle between the two canyons at 7.8 miles.

The route follows a short side canyon down to the floor of Granite Canyon, guarded by great spires and rock columns. From here turn left for a short 0.5-mile round-trip exploration of the narrow upper reaches of Granite Canyon. You'll quickly come to an 8-foot dry fall that can be readily climbed. But the next chokestone, only 50 yards beyond, is more difficult. This is a good turnaround point for the hike back down Granite Canyon. Granite Canyon is steeper and more bouldery than Through Canyon but can be easily negotiated on a mostly sandy wash. After another mile the canyon widens to a valley. Low granite walls on the left side lead up to a colorful red chasm. Overall, Granite is a wonderful contrast to Through Canyon, especially in the upper end, where moderate bouldering and narrow canyons are true delights. Along the way you'll see broken quartz monzonite that is unlike most other places in the park.

After exiting the wide mouth of Granite Canyon at 11 miles, continue down the wash toward the southern edge of the Confidence Hills. When you reach the base

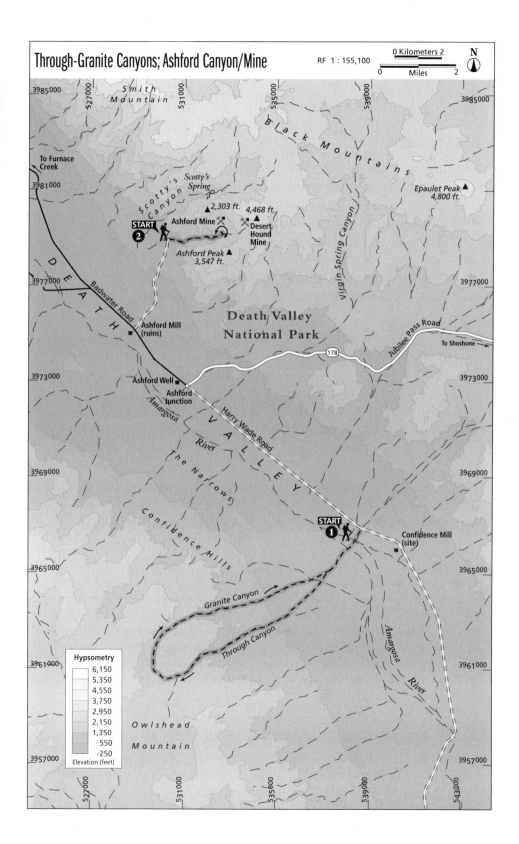

Through-Granite Canyons; Ashford Canyon/Mine

RF 1 : 155,100

0 Kilometers 2

0 Miles 2

N

Smith Mountain

Black Mountains

To Furnace Creek

Scotty's Canyon

Scotty's Spring

▲ 2,303 ft.   4,468 ft. ▲

Ashford Mine

Epaulet Peak ▲
4,800 ft.

Desert Hound Mine

Ashford Peak ▲
3,547 ft.

Virgin Spring Canyon

START 2

DEATH

Badwater Road

Ashford Mill (ruins)

Death Valley
National Park

Jubilee Pass Road

To Shoshone

178

Ashford Well

Ashford Junction

Amargosa River

VALLEY

Harry Wade Road

The Narrows

Confidence Hills

START 1

Confidence Mill (site)

Granite Canyon

Through Canyon

Amargosa River

Hypsometry

| 6,150 |
| 5,350 |
| 4,550 |
| 3,750 |
| 2,950 |
| 2,150 |
| 1,350 |
| 550 |
| -250 |

Elevation (feet)

Owlshead
Mountain

of these brown hills in the serpentine steep-walled wash, you'll intersect the stem of this "lollipop" loop. Roughly retrace the first 2 miles of the route in a northeasterly direction back to Confidence Wash, thereby completing this adventuresome 15-mile exploration.

Miles and Directions

0.0 Start at the parking area at Confidence Wash on Harry Wade Road.

2.0 Arrive at the southern edge of the Confidence Hills.

4.3 Arrive at the mouth of Through Canyon.

7.4 Angle right (north) to the Granite-Through Canyon divide.

7.8 Arrive at the divide between the Granite and Through Canyons.

11.0 Arrive at the mouth of Granite Canyon.

13.0 Arrive again at the southern edge of the Confidence Hills.

15.0 Return to the parking area at Confidence Wash on Harry Wade Road.

2 Ashford Canyon/Mine

An extensive mine site with several intact buildings lies up a remote and narrow canyon. The rocky mining road has become a hiking trail, leading to the historic early-twentieth-century mine site.

See map on page 23.
Start: About 45 miles south of Furnace Creek.
Distance: 3 miles out and back.
Approximate hiking time: 2 to 3 hours.
Difficulty: Moderate.
Trail surface: Rocky trail.

Seasons: October through April.
USGS topo map: Shore Line Butte-CA (1:24,000).
Trail contact: Furnace Creek Visitor Center & Museum (see appendix D).

Finding the trailhead: From California Highway 127, 1.7 miles north of Shoshone, turn left (west) on California Highway 178 (East Side Badwater Road/Jubilee Pass Road), which leads to the park boundary. After entering the park, drive 25.1 miles to the signed Ashford Mill Road on the left, 1.9 miles north of Ashford Junction and 26.9 miles south of Badwater. Turn right (east) onto the unsigned Ashford Canyon Road leading northeast directly across from the Ashford Mill site. If coming from the north, drive 44.5 miles south of Furnace Creek on Badwater Road to Ashford Canyon Road on the left. Follow this four-wheel-drive road for 3 miles to the mouth of Ashford Canyon. Park and hike from here.

The Hike

The Ashford (Golden Treasure) Mine was discovered in 1907 and was sold a few years later to supply gold ore to the Ashford Mill. The early years were probably its

Ashford Mine buildings 1.6 miles up Ashford Canyon are surrounded by high, rugged peaks.

most productive, since the mine sold for more money than it ultimately yielded. The inefficiency of the mill was at least partly to blame.

From the mouth of the canyon, the old mining trail climbs steeply up the left side of the deep, narrow Ashford Canyon. Rock slides and erosion are gradually erasing any sign of the trail as nature reclaims the land. But there is still enough evidence of rock construction and built-up roadbeds to make this route fairly easy to follow.

After dropping into the canyon bottom, the road crosses the wash several times. Several steep sections of slanted rock are avoided as the trail pitches right or left. Huge round mine timbers and scattered diggings are found about halfway up. At 1.3 miles the road crosses the wash and contours to the left around the slope, climbs slightly, and then drops to the mining camp.

The buildings are still somewhat intact, containing some of the furniture and appliances used by the miners. Although they made no effort to clean up their trash, one has to marvel at the incredible determination and optimism the miners must have had to carve such an extensive operation out of such difficult terrain. The miners sure had a view in this southern stretch of the Black Mountains, with Ashford

Peak soaring to the south and the rugged canyon below opening to the Owlshead and Panamint Mountains westward. Retrace your route to complete this 3-mile round-trip exploration of some of Death Valley's mining history.

Miles and Directions

0.0   Start at the trailhead at the mouth of Ashford Canyon.

0.3   Climb out of the wash (right), bypassing a dry fall/rock slide.

0.5   The trail follows the wash up a rough, rocky surface.

1.3   The trail crosses the wash and climbs the slope to the left.

1.5   Arrive at Ashford (Golden Treasure) Mine.

3.0   Return to the trailhead by the same route.

Options: Other nearby mining sites include the Desert Hound Mine high on the mountaintop a mile to the northeast, and Scotty's Canyon, which is the next canyon to the north a couple of miles. With the aid of a topo map, a 4-mile round-trip hike to Scotty's Canyon is well worth exploring. The canyon has perennial water from a spring.

3 Sidewinder Canyon

This steep, rugged canyon opens to grand vistas of the floor of Death Valley. The canyon out-and-back hike has good highway access, requiring no four-wheel-drive vehicle. Narrow tunnels and sheer rock slots require moderate scrambling to dramatic views of Death Valley. Special attractions include several short slot side canyons that invite further exploration. The canyon also lies within bighorn-sheep habitat.

Start: About 34 miles south of Furnace Creek.
Distance: 4.6-mile out and back in main canyon plus short side hikes in slot canyons.
Approximate hiking time: 3 to 4 hours.
Difficulty: Moderate.
Trail surface: Dirt path, rocky alluvial fan, with short stretches of cross-country and moderate rock climbing.
Seasons: November through April.
USGS topo map: Gold Valley-CA (1:24,000).
Trail contact: Furnace Creek Visitor Center & Museum (see appendix D).

Finding the trailhead: From the Furnace Creek Visitor Center, drive 1 mile south to the junction of California Highways 178 (Badwater Road) and 190; turn south on Badwater Road and drive 33 miles to an unsigned dirt road that leads 0.2 mile left (southeast). This turn is easy to miss, but it is just before the highway makes a half-circle to the west (toward the valley). Proceed on the dirt road for 0.2 mile to a T that contains a short stretch of pavement. Turn right on

The narrows of Sidewinder Canyon at 2.2 miles. ▶

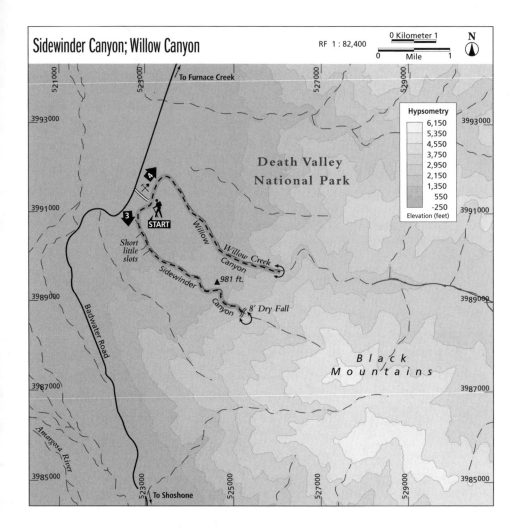

RF 1 : 82,400

0 Kilometer 1

0   Mile   1

N

To Furnace Creek

Death Valley
National Park

Hypsometry

| 6,150 |
| 5,350 |
| 4,550 |
| 3,750 |
| 2,950 |
| 2,150 |
| 1,350 |
| 550 |
| -250 |

Elevation (feet)

Willow

Short
little
slots

Willow Creek
Canyon

Sidewinder

▲981 ft.

Canyon

8' Dry Fall

Badwater Road

B l a c k
M o u n t a i n s

Amargosa River

To Shoshone

the T and drive to its end in less than 0.1 mile and park; this is the trailhead for both the Willow Canyon hike and the Sidewinder Canyon hike. The mouth of Sidewinder Canyon cannot be seen from the parking area, but it is straight south about 0.3 mile up and across a rocky alluvial fan.

The Hike

This excursion into the lower end of rugged Sidewinder Canyon provides a solid introduction to the wild canyon country of the Black Mountains.

Begin by hiking 0.3 mile southward across a rocky alluvial fan to the mouth of Sidewinder Canyon. The canyon opens to a broad wash exactly at sea level, but still high above the salt flats to the northeast. At 1 mile the graveled wash widens dramatically to a huge semicircle presenting a grand view of Death Valley and the

Panamint Range beyond. A narrow, dark, cavelike slot canyon leads up to the right, enticing you to take a short side trip. At 1.2 miles another tight slot canyon enters from the right. This side canyon is also short and well worth a quick exploratory look. Thereafter, turn right up the main wash.

Continuing up Sidewinder, the wide wash soon funnels into a more narrow canyon. At 1.8 miles more "slots" appear in the rock with another slanted rock drop-off. Here the conglomerate canyon walls are steep with deep overhangs and little alcoves along the narrow passageway. This portion of the canyon is bound by high rugged mountains with markedly higher rhyolite walls along the face of the main uplift.

At around 2 miles the canyon hosts a series of steep, slanted rocks that can be readily climbed and descended with moderate levels of skill and agility. This stretch of Sidewinder has impressive slots in the rock, with narrows intensifying the canyon experience.

At 2.3 miles an 8-foot dry fall is encountered. An experienced rock climber could scale this dry waterfall and continue up the canyon, but most people would have a difficult time pulling themselves over the exposed ledge. The base of this short waterfall is actually an excellent turnaround point for this stimulating 4.6 mile round-trip exploration of Sidewinder Canyon.

Miles and Directions

0.0 The trailhead is just east of the Badwater Road.

0.3 Arrive at the mouth of Sidewinder Canyon.

0.9 A large side canyon enters from the right.

1.0 A gravelly wash widens to a huge circular amphitheater.

1.2 A narrow slot side canyon enters from the right.

1.8–2.2 More "slots" appear in the canyon, with slanted rock to traverse.

2.3 An 8-foot dry fall is encountered in Sidewinder Canyon (turnaround point).

4.6 Return to the trailhead.

4 Willow Canyon

Seasonal waterfalls provide a suitable home for bighorn sheep in Willow Canyon.

See map on page 28.
Start: About 34 miles south of Furnace Creek.
Length: 5 miles out and back.
Approximate hiking time: 2 to 3 hours.
Difficulty: Moderate.

Trail surface: Sandy trail with rocky sections.
Seasons: November through April.
USGS topo map: Gold Valley-CA (1:24,000).
Trail contact: Furnace Creek Visitor Center & Museum (see appendix D).

Finding the trailhead: From the California Highways 190 and 178 junction at the Furnace Creek Inn, go south on Badwater Road (CA 178) for 33 miles to an unsigned dirt road on your left. Drive 0.2 mile to a T-shaped paved parking area adjacent to a gravel pit used during the construction of the East Road in Death Valley. The unmarked trail leaves from the northwest corner of the T lot. This parking area is also the trailhead for Sidewinder Canyon.

The Hike

Although the ratio of hiking the alluvial fan to hiking in the canyon may seem lopsided, this hike features a gem of a canyon. Clearly a bighorn-sheep playground, Willow Canyon cuts short your visit at a 70-foot wall with a spectacular ribbon waterfall in season. Prior to that obstacle the canyon winds its narrow way like a street in a medieval city through sheer rhyolite walls, with a tinkling stream intermittently flowing down its center. Small falls, a shelf fall, and finally a long ribbon fall make the passage of the stream a delightful symphony of watery music.

The trip to this canyon follows a use trail that seeks the sandy sections of the fan and wash. Upon leaving the parking area, head northeast, staying below the eroding ash hillsides and their alluvial fans. The sloping forms of these latter features are the southern boundary of the Willow Canyon wash. Beyond their tilting faces, to the northeast, is a vertical wall of the same volcanic ash. This vertical wall is the northern boundary of Willow Canyon wash, and it is clearly seen as you wind your way up the fan following the sandy use trail, which takes you into the wash and on to the canyon itself.

Since you cannot see the canyon from the parking area—only the notch in the mountains beyond the volcanic ash hills suggests it—it is an exciting and abrupt change when the wash enters the canyon. Sheer rust-colored rhyolite walls tower above the gray gravel of the canyon floor. From the brightness of the open wash in the valley, you are suddenly enshrouded in cool shadows. The warm wind of the valley becomes a cool breeze within the canyon walls. And, if the season is right, the sound of running water cascading over the eroding canyon floor breaks the silence.

Ribbon falls punctuate the end of the Willow Canyon hike. ▶

Plentiful sheep sign (tracks, scat, etc.) confirms that this is bighorn-sheep habitat, but it is unlikely that you will spot these elusive animals. If lucky enough to do so, please report sheep sightings to park personnel at the visitor center. The presence of water in Willow Canyon makes it a popular spot for the sheep.

Even in season, the stream in Willow Canyon is intermittent. At times it disappears underground, only to reappear again as another waterfall. Thus playing a hide-and-seek game, the stream brings visual and aural delight to the hiker. At 2.4 miles the stream drops over an extended shelf of rock in a 3-foot fall (easily climbed via a rock-step to the side). Immediately above the shelf, the stream vanishes again. The canyon narrows to less than 15 feet in width as the water-polished walls seem to close the canyon completely. Emerging from the narrows 0.1 mile later, you are confronted with the barricade that terminates the hike: a 70-foot sheer fall rising above you. The stream, when running, comes over this precipice in a silky ribbon. When dry, the fall is also striking for its marbleized water-smoothed surface.

The return trip from the canyon involves retracing your steps. Leaving the canyon's watery world is done with reluctance; Willow Canyon resembles an oasis at the southern edge of Death Valley.

Miles and Directions

0.0–0.7 Use the trail across the sandy sections of the alluvial fan to the mouth of the wash.

0.7–2.1 Use the trail up the wash to the canyon mouth.

2.1–2.5 Hike the canyon trail to the dry/wet fall (depends upon season).

5.0 Return to the trailhead.

5 Dante's View

This short, easy hike offers magnificent panoramic views of the highest and lowest points in the continental United States. Surrounded by some of the most dramatic and colorful relief found anywhere, you also enjoy the astounding vertical relief of being nearly 6,000 feet directly above the lowest spot in the nation at Badwater.

Start: About 24 miles south of Furnace Creek.
Distance: 1 mile out and back.
Approximate hiking time: Less than 1 hour.
Difficulty: Easy.
Trail surface: Clear trail; paved road access.

Seasons: October through June.
USGS topo map: Dantes View-CA (1:24,000).
Trail contact: Furnace Creek Visitor Center & Museum (see appendix D).

Dante's View provides breathtaking perspective on the amazing vertical relief between Badwater at minus 282 feet and snow-capped 11,049-foot Telescope Peak in the distance.

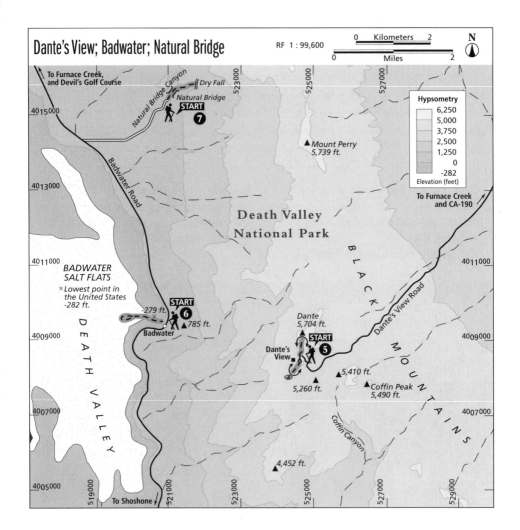

Finding the trailhead: From California Highway 190, 11.9 miles southeast of the Furnace Creek Visitor Center and 18 miles west of Death Valley Junction, turn south on the signed Dante's View Road (paved, all-weather). Drive 13.2 miles on this steep, winding road to its end at the Dante's View parking area. The unsigned path to Dante Point takes off to the north from the parking area and is clearly visible from the parking area as it climbs toward Dante Point.

The Hike

If at all possible, take this hike in the early morning so that the sun is at your back for better photography and for enhanced enjoyment of the superlative vistas and astounding 5,704-foot drop to the salt flats of Badwater, which sit at 282 feet below sea level. The temperature at Dante's View averages 25 degrees cooler than that of Badwater. This exposed location is usually windy, necessitating a windbreak garment during the hike.

This lofty vantage point in the Black Mountains enables you to almost see, or at least visualize, how the mountains are both slowly moving to the left (south) and rising relative to the surrounding terrain. Looking across Death Valley to the highest point in the park, 11,049-foot Telescope Peak, it is easy to note the major vegetative life zones stretching westward like a giant map. Bristlecone and limber pines thrive high in the Panamint Range. Below is the piñon-juniper zone. Dante's View is situated in a hotter, drier midslope of blackbrush and sage. Floods from the mountains result in graveled fans with spreading root species such as creosote bush. Fresh water displaces salt from the edges of fans, allowing mesquite to grow. Pickleweed gains a foothold in the brackish water below these edges. The muddy tans and grays of the valley floor grade into white beds of almost pure salt—a chemical desert.

From the parking lot, hike north along the road for 0.1 mile to where the Dante Point trail begins a fairly steep climb up the hill. Soon it winds to the left (west) and contours gently along the west slope of the mountain. This contour route provides an even more impressive view down to Badwater, with an almost overwhelming sense of vertical relief—more than a mile straight down! At 0.3 mile the trail intersects the summit ridge, then climbs the short distance to the 5,704-foot high point. Although unofficial, the trail is clear, well defined, and easy to follow. Return the way you came to complete this 1-mile out-and-back ridge walk—and don't forget your camera.

For a slightly different and highly worthwhile perspective, hike a well-used path 0.25 mile southwest of the parking area. The rock outcropping at the point of the ridge is especially welcome as a windbreak for setting up a tripod for early-morning photography.

6 Badwater

A perfectly flat hike on a boardwalk leads you onto the salt flats at the lowest point in the United States. This vast bed of salt lies 282 feet below sea level.

See map on page 34.
Start: About 17 miles south of Furnace Creek.
Distance: 1 mile out and back.
Approximate hiking time: Less than 1 hour.
Difficulty: Easy.

Trail surface: Clear salt flat.
Seasons: Late October through March.
USGS topo map: Badwater-CA (1:24,000).
Trail contact: Furnace Creek Visitor Center & Museum (see appendix D).

The view to the northeast from the salt flats of Badwater—282 feet below sea level.

Finding the trailhead: On Badwater Road, 16.7 miles south of the California Highway 190/Badwater (California Highway 178) junction at the Furnace Creek Inn, the signed parking area for Badwater is on the west side of the road.

The Hike

As bleak as it looks, a hike onto the salt flats at Badwater is arguably the ultimate Death Valley experience. If you have been to Dante's View or Telescope Peak, you probably saw the human "ants" on the white expanse of valley floor and wondered what could be so fascinating. Here you will find individuals, especially families, cavorting like they're at the beach or enjoying a spring snow. Just being out here on the boardwalk gives a genuine sense of the enormity of the salt flats.

The hike begins at the parking area beneath the cliffs that soar up to Dante's View, 5,755 feet above. There's a SEA LEVEL sign on the cliff face, high above Bad-water, making very clear what minus-282 feet represent. Walk out to the salt flats on the boardwalk. Getting away from the highway is essential to get a sense of the magnitude of the salt flats.

Here fresh salt crystals are forming as groundwater percolates to the surface, bringing salt that crystallizes as the water hastily evaporates—chemistry in action. If you sit on the edge of the boardwalk and study the miniaturized terrain of the salt flats, you will find yourself among tiny salt pinnacles, a miniature mountainous world at the bottom of this mountainous basin. In close contact with the surface, you will also discover that salt is a tough commodity. The white flooring of the flats is only inches thick, but surprisingly firm. Salt's power as an erosive force is noteworthy in this desert, where it functions much like frost heaves and ice do in a wet climate. Salt crystals grow and force apart boulders, breaking them down to be further eroded by wind and water.

Above the microworld of salt, the world of Death Valley soars. To the west is Telescope Peak (11,049 feet), the highest point in the park, less than 20 miles away. The difference in elevation between Badwater and Telescope Peak is one of the largest in the United States.

A hike at Badwater is an essential introduction to the expanse of the valley floor. The emigrants and the miners who lived in this environment were a tough lot.

7 Natural Bridge

An easy, sloped canyon leads to a natural bridge that arches over the trail. The geological phenomena—faults, slipfaulting, chutes and dry fall, natural arch formation—are explained at the trailhead exhibits.

See map on page 34.
Start: About 13 miles south of Furnace Creek.
Distance: 2 miles out and back.
Approximate hiking time: 1 to 2 hours.
Difficulty: Easy.
Trail surface: Sandy canyon bottom.

Seasons: October through April.
USGS topo map: Devils Golf Course-CA (1:24,000).
Trail contact: Furnace Creek Visitor Center (see appendix D).

Finding the trailhead: From the intersection of California Highway 190 and Badwater Road (California Highway 178) in Furnace Creek, drive south on Badwater Road for 14.1 miles. Turn left (east) on the signed dirt road and drive 1.5 miles to the Natural Bridge parking area. The road is washboardy and rough but is suitable for standard two-wheel-drive vehicles. The trail begins behind the information kiosk.

The Hike

Death Valley's fascinating geologic history is featured on the kiosk at the trailhead of the Natural Bridge hike. Bedding and slipfaulting are explained on the board, so the canyon's display is even more impressive. Likewise, differential erosion is explained and illustrated, preparing you for the bridge. Fault caves, metamorphic layers of the Artist's Drive Formation, and mud drips are other topics covered in this condensed version of physical geology. The kiosk is worth a lengthy pause before embarking on the hike.

The canyon floor consists of loose gravel; that feature plus its sharp slope suggests this is a relatively young canyon. The Death Valley floor continues to subside while the Funeral Mountains rise. Geologic forces are still busy here.

The trail begins through deeply eroded volcanic ash and pumice canyon walls. The canyon gradually narrows. At 0.4 mile the bridge stretches over the canyon bottom. An ancient streambed is visible to the north of the bridge, where the floods swept around this more resistant section of strata before the pothole beneath it gave way to form the natural bridge.

Beyond the bridge, mud drips, slip faults, and fault caves appear on your journey uphill, reinforcing the information you picked up at the kiosk. A dry fall at 0.8 mile can be climbed with moderate effort, but a 20-foot dry fall blocks travel at 1 mile.

Retracing your steps down the canyon reveals even more examples of geology in action. The shifting lighting creates iridescent colors. Traveling in the same

The natural bridge—monumental gateway to the upper canyon. ▶

direction as the powerful flash floods and their load of scouring debris emphasizes the impact of water in this arid environment.

Miles and Directions

0.0 The trail heads northwest from the parking area.

0.4 Arrive at the natural bridge over the trail.

0.8 Carefully climb the smaller dry fall.

1.0 Where a 20-foot dry fall blocks the canyon, return to the trailhead.

2.0 Arrive back at the parking area.

8 Desolation Canyon

Desolation Canyon is a highly scenic but less crowded alternative to the nearby Golden Canyon. This short hike features moderate canyoneering to a high pass overlooking the Artist's Drive Formation. The deep, narrow, colorful canyon provides a feeling of solitude, with broad vistas from the overlook.

Start: About 5 miles south of Furnace Creek.
Distance: 5.2 miles out and back.
Approximate hiking time: 2 hours.
Difficulty: Moderate.
Trail surface: Clear wash with 3 short rock pitches.

Seasons: Early November to mid-April.
USGS topo map: Furnace Creek-CA (1:24,000).
Trail contact: Furnace Creek Visitor Center & Museum (see appendix D).

Finding the trailhead: From the Death Valley Visitor Center in Furnace Creek, drive south 1.2 miles to the junction of California Highway 190 and Badwater Road (location of the Furnace Creek Inn); turn right (south) onto Badwater Road (California Highway 178) and drive 3.9 miles to the unsigned parking area, which is to the left along the east side of the highway. The old road was washed out by the big thunderstorm flood of August 2004 and might not be rebuilt. Hike 1 mile to the end of the old road. Desolation Canyon is to the immediate left (northeast) of the old road. Follow one of several well-worn paths that lead northeast over the low ridge to the broad lower end of Desolation Canyon.

The Hike

This is an enjoyable and highly scenic canyon hike for anyone, but it is especially appreciated by those without a four-wheel-drive vehicle in that access is just off the paved highway. Despite its proximity to both the Badwater Road and Artist's Drive, the narrow canyon provides a deep feeling of intimacy and solitude. The entire out-and-back trip provides a superb opportunity to observe the dynamics of badlands erosion, which is everywhere, from mud-filled gullies to bizarre eroded shapes overlooking the canyon.

Hiking up the wash from the mouth of Desolation Canyon.

Because Desolation Canyon involves a short hike at low elevation, the recommended time of day for the hike is mid- to late afternoon when the cooler shadows fill the canyon. Upon return, late afternoon to early evening, brilliant light can be spectacular on the multicolored east-facing slopes above the canyon.

The main Desolation Canyon is just over the low ridge to the north from the end of the old road. Upon reaching the canyon in 1.1 mile, turn right and head up the wide wash that climbs gently to the first canyon junction at 1.3 mile, staying to the right. Continue right at the next junction at 1.4 mile. At 1.5 mile the canyon narrows with even narrower side draws. The next 0.1 mile brings a couple of stair-step rocks that are easy to climb, before the canyon again widens. At 2.1 miles what appears to be the main canyon to the left ends at a dry waterfall another 0.1 mile up. Continuing up the more narrow canyon to the right ends at a steep, unstable rock chute at 2.5 miles. This is a good turnaround point.

If you've still got the urge and energy to explore, climb up to the right on loose, deep gravel to the 740-foot elevation overlook at 2.6 miles. This relatively lofty vantage point provides a spectacular view of the varied colors of the Artist's Drive

Desolation Canyon; Golden Canyon/Gower Gulch Loop; Pyramid Canyon; Harmony Borax Works; Upper Hole-in-the-Wall

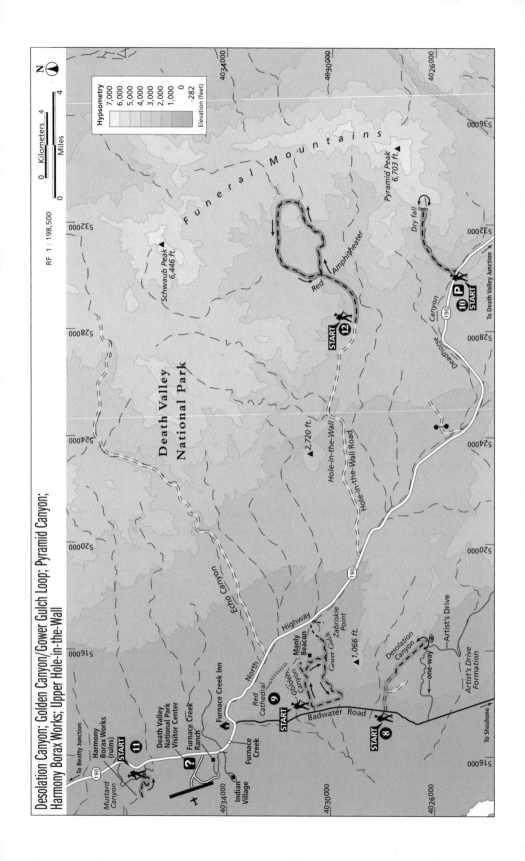

RF 1 : 198,500

Hypsometry

7,000
6,000
5,000
4,000
3,000
2,000
1,000
0
-282

Elevation (feet)

0   Kilometers   4

0   Miles   4

N

Funeral Mountains

Schwaub Peak ▲
6,446 ft.

Pyramid Peak ▲
6,703 ft.

Death Valley National Park

Red Amphitheater

START 12

Dry fall

10 P START

To Death Valley Junction

Deadhorse Canyon

▲ 2,720 ft.

Hole-in-the-Wall

Hole-in-the-Wall Road

190

Echo Canyon

Furnace Creek Inn

North Highway

Manly Beacon

Zabriskie Point

▲ 1,066 ft.

Red Cathedral

Golden Canyon

Gower Gulch

START 9

Desolation Canyon

one-way

Artist's Drive

Artist's Drive Formation

To Beatty Junction

Harmony Borax Works (ruins)

START 11

Mustard Canyon

Death Valley National Park Visitor Center

Furnace Creek Ranch

?

Furnace Creek

Indian Village

Badwater Road

START 8

To Shoshone

Formation to the south. From this point the Artist's Drive road is only about 0.3 mile west. Return by way of Desolation Canyon to complete this colorful 5.2-mile round-trip badlands/canyon excursion.

Miles and Directions

0.0   Start at the trailhead/parking area.

1.1   At the intersection with the Desolation Canyon wash, turn right up the canyon.

1.3   Where the canyon splits, stay right.

1.4   At the canyon junction, stay right up the main wash.

1.6   The canyon steepens with moderate scrambling.

1.7   The canyon widens to a junction. Go right up the steeper, less colorful canyon with more stair-step rocks.

2.1   At the canyon junction, stay right up a narrow gully.

2.5   The hike ends where the canyon reaches a steep chute. This is the turnaround point for the moderate hike.

2.6   Scramble up a very steep, unstable slope (right) to the overlook.

5.2   Return to the trailhead via the same route.

9   Golden Canyon/Gower Gulch Loop

A fascinating journey through geologic time passes through rocks of different ages as the elevation increases then loops back down to the floor of Death Valley past borax-mine tunnels. The first section is an educational geology nature trail. The scenery of the extended trip includes a colorful lake bed, exposed strata and alluvial-fan formations, and spectacular scenery of the Panamint Range from below Zabriskie Point.

See map on page 42.
Start: About 3 miles south of Furnace Creek.
Distance: 6.5-mile loop (including 2 short side trips).
Approximate hiking time: 3 to 5 hours.
Difficulty: Moderate.

Trail surface: Sandy trail and rocky wash.
Seasons: November through April.
USGS topo map: Furnace Creek-CA (1:24,000).
Trail contact: Furnace Creek Visitor Center & Museum (see appendix D).

Finding the trailhead: From the north on California Highway 190, 1.2 miles south of the Furnace Creek Visitor Center, head south on Badwater Road (California Highway 178). After 2 miles, turn left into the Golden Canyon parking area/trailhead on the east side of the road. From the south, turn west on CA 178 2 miles north of the small town of Shoshone and continue into the park. From Ashford Junction, continue north on Badwater Road. The signed Golden Canyon parking area is 14.4 miles north of Badwater and can be seen just off the highway to the right (east).

The sharp point of Manly Beacon (left) is complemented by the dramatic amber face of the Red Cathedral (right background).

The Hike

An excellent interpretive trail guide to this Golden Canyon nature trail is available for 50 cents at the Golden Canyon trailhead. Ten stops in this geology guide are keyed to numbered posts along the trail.

Golden Canyon was once accessed by paved road. Then in February 1976 a four-day storm caused 2.3 inches of rain to fall on nearby Furnace Creek—one of the driest places on earth where no rain fell during all of 1929 and 1953. Runoff from the torrential cloudburst undermined and washed out the pavement so that today Golden Canyon is a wonderful place for hikers only. This pattern of drought and torrents follows countless periods of flash floods, shattering rock slides, and a wetter era when the alluvial fan was preceded by an ancient shallow sea—a land in constant flux. In the winter of 2004, heavy rains caused flooding, washing out sections of Badwater Road and further eroding these canyons and gulches.

At stop 2 it is easy to see how the canyon was carved out of an old alluvial fan made up of volcanic rock that predates the origin of Death Valley some three million years ago. Layers in the rock tell the tale of periodic floods over the eons. Just above, the canyon displays tilted bands of rock caused by faulting where huge blocks of the earth's crust slid past one another. As you proceed up the canyon, you are literally passing through geologic time. The Furnace Creek Formation is the combination over time of sediments from a lake bed that dates back around nine million years. Ripple marks of water lapping over the sandy lake bed hardened into stone as the climate warmed and are evident on the tilted rock. Weathering and the effects of thermal water produced the splash of vivid colors seen today.

Mountain building to the west gradually produced a more arid climate, causing the lake to dry up. At the same time the land tilted due to the widening and sinking of Death Valley and the uplift of the Black Mountains. Dark lava from eruptions of three million to five million years ago slowed down erosion, explaining why Manly Beacon juts so far above the surrounding badlands. These stark badlands rising above the canyon at mile 0.5 are the result of rapid runoff from storms on erodable, almost impermeable rocks.

Several narrow side canyons invite short explorations on the way up Golden Canyon, particularly opposite stop 2, and to the left and just above stops 6 and 7.

The nature trail ends at stop 10, about 1 mile up the canyon at an elevation of 140 feet. For a 0.8-mile round-trip to the base of the Red Cathedral, continue straight ahead up the broken pavement, past the old parking area, to a narrow notch, directly below the looming presence of the cathedral from where the highest point in the park—Telescope Peak—can be seen in the far distance.

Red Cathedral was once part of an active alluvial fan, outwashed from the Black Mountains to the south. The bright red results from the weathering of iron to produce the rust of iron oxide. The cliff faces are made up of the more resistant red rock crowning softer yellow lake deposits.

Upon returning to stop 10 (mile 1.8), follow the signed trail to the left (coming down) up a steep gully well marked with trailposts. The trail climbs across badlands beneath the imposing sandstone jaw of Manly Beacon. At 2.3 miles a high ridge saddle is reached below Manly Beacon. Follow the markers down a side gully to a wash/trail junction at 2.6 miles. The left-hand wash leads eastward up to Zabriskie Point. The right-hand wash/trail descends west to Gower Gulch. If you walk up the main wash, you will quickly come to the artificial cut made in the rock wall to divert Furnace Creek through Gower Gulch. This has resulted in speeding up erosion in the gulch. Note the gray color of the rocks on the bottom of the drainage washed in from Furnace Creek, contrasting with the red and yellow badlands.

Gower Gulch is partially the result of human construction to protect Furnace Creek from serious flooding. For a short side trip toward Zabriskie Point, turn left at the junction and follow the markers for about 0.5 mile from where you can select an excellent overlook of Zabriskie Point, the surrounding badlands, Death Valley, and the distant Panamint Range. Zabriskie Point is another 0.7 mile and 200 feet above and is accessible by road from the other side. It does indeed provide one of the most magnificent views in all of Death Valley, but its proximity to a paved road may detract from the hiking experience on the Golden-Gower loop. Thus, the overlook below Zabriskie Point is recommended as the turnaround point for a scenic side trip. Zabriskie Point is a popular starting point for those hiking 3 miles downhill through Gower Gulch then across to the mouth of Golden Canyon.

Back at the trail junction (mile 3.6), there is no marker post leading the way toward Gower Gulch. Simply continue down the wash toward wide, gray Gower Gulch, which drops below mounds of golden badlands. At 3.9 miles a side wash intersects the main wash; continue downward to the right. Early-day miners in search of borax have pocketed the walls of Gower Gulch with tunnels. These small openings are unsecured and potentially dangerous. A mile down, the wide gravel wash bends sharply to the left, narrowing dramatically with the bedding and faulting of red and green rock. The canyon floor then quickly drops 40 feet to below sea level.

At 5.2 miles the wash meets a 30-foot dry fall. A good use trail curves around the rock face to the right. From here the faint but easy-to-follow trail heads north 1.3 miles along the base of the mountains paralleling the highway back to the Golden Canyon parking area, thereby completing the basic 4.7-mile loop with an additional 1.8 miles of side trips.

Miles and Directions

0.0 Start at the Golden Canyon nature trail trailhead at 160 feet below sea level.

1.0 The nature trail ends at stop 10. Begin the 0.8-mile side trip to the base of the Red Cathedral here.

1.8 Back to stop 10 and the beginning of the trail toward Manly Beacon.

2.3 Arrive at the high point of the trail below Manly Beacon.

2.6 Arrive at the trail/wash junction between Gower Gulch and Zabriskie Point.

3.1 Arrive at the overlook below Zabriskie Point.

3.6 Get back to the trail/wash junction and begin the hike down Gower Gulch.

5.2 Gower Gulch reaches a 30-foot dry fall. Take the trail around to the right.

6.5 Complete the loop back at the Golden Canyon trailhead.

10 Pyramid Canyon

This is an easily accessible, waterless, out-and-back canyon hike with layered color-banded mountains. The mountains close into a narrow, dark chasm that is blocked in several places by boulders.

See map on page 42.
Start: About 14 miles southeast of Furnace Creek.
Distance: 4 miles out and back.
Approximate hiking time: 2 to 3 hours.
Difficulty: Moderate.
Trail surface: No trail but a sandy wash with loose gravel and moderate bouldering.
Seasons: October through April.
USGS topo maps: Ryan-CA and Echo Canyon-CA (1:24,000).
Trail contact: Furnace Creek Visitor Center & Museum (see appendix D).

Finding the trailhead: From the Furnace Creek Visitor Center, drive about 14 miles east on North Highway (California Highway 190). Shortly after passing an information kiosk/pay phone, you'll leave the park boundary on the south side of the highway. Drive another 1.1 miles and look to the north side of the highway for a prominent wash. The trailhead is unsigned, but there is a wide spot alongside the highway on the north side for parking.

The Hike

Some of the limestone in the surrounding Furnace Creek Formation is probably travertine that was laid down by volcanic hot springs. Travertine Point rises just east of the trailhead on the south side of the canyon. Pyramid Canyon is not an official place name on the map but is used here to identify the hike. When viewed from the mouth of Pyramid Canyon, the imposing, aptly named massif of Pyramid Peak dominates the skyline to the northeast. After 0.25 mile you'll come to an old rusted car body halfway buried in the wash—proof positive that you're in the right canyon. Barrel cacti dot the surrounding alluvial-fan conglomerate.

Continue hiking up the wide wash to narrows that define a dramatic gateway beyond. At 1.5 miles the canyon is blocked by a boulder, with dark cliffs ahead. Look back to the southwest for a great view of Telescope Peak. Climb to the left up a slanted rock to get around the boulder. At mile 1.7 reddish dark cliff walls soar hundreds of feet as the canyon again closes in. The next two boulder blockages occur in quick succession and can be readily climbed. But the fourth blockage at 2 miles is impassable. A gigantic chokestone sits atop a dry fall bound by sheer limestone cliffs. An alcove overhang juts out from the cliff high above the dry fall on the north side of the canyon. Retrace your route to complete this 4-mile round-trip canyon "teaser."

Miles and Directions

0.0 Start at the unsigned trailhead/parking area along the north side of the highway (2,560 feet elevation).

0.25 Look for the old half-buried car body in the wash.

1.5 At the first rock blockage, the canyon narrows.

1.7 Arrive at the second rock blockage.

1.8 This is the third rock blockage.

2.0 Turn around upon reaching the dry fall/chokestone.

4.0 Return to the trailhead.

Option: For added variety during the return route, look for a low ridge on the right side of the broad wash, about 0.5-mile below the dry-fall turnaround. Angle around the ridge and head up the left (west) fork for about 0.4-mile to a 30-foot dry fall. This two-pronged exploration of Pyramid Canyon adds about 0.8-mile round-trip to the hike.

11 Harmony Borax Works

This short hike on a loop trail leads to a nineteenth-century industrial site on the valley floor. The endless salt flats are an overwhelming sight.

See map on page 42.
Start: About 1.5 miles north of Furnace Creek.
Distance: 1 mile out and back.
Approximate hiking time: Less than 1 hour.
Difficulty: Easy.
Trail surface: Asphalt walkway to Harmony Borax Works (wheelchair accessible); sandy trail to overlook and to salt flats.

Seasons: October through March.
USGS topo maps: West of Furnace Creek-CA and Furnace Creek-CA (1:24,000).
Trail contact: Furnace Creek Visitor Center & Museum (see appendix D).

Finding the trailhead: The trailhead for the Harmony Borax Works Trail is 1.3 miles north of the park visitor center at Furnace Creek via California Highway 190. The 0.2-mile road on the left is signed. The asphalt walkway leads west of the parking area.

The Hike

This desolate site was the scene of frenzied activity from 1883 to 1888, not in the pursuit of gold like so much of the other mining activity, but of borax. Used in ceramics and glass as well as soap and detergent, borax was readily available here in Death Valley. Borax prices were highly mercurial due to soaring supply and moderate demand in the nineteenth century, so the industry was plagued by sharp

A 20-mule team wagon stands at the historic Harmony Borax Works trail.

boom and bust cycles. Here at the Harmony Works, the years of prosperity were typically brief.

Chinese laborers hauled the borate sludge in from the flats on sledges to the processing plant, remains of which are the focal point of this hike. There the borate was boiled down and hauled 165 miles across the desert to Mojave by the famed twenty-mule teams. One of the wagons that made this journey stands below the borax plant. Although the works were in operation only from October to June, working conditions for man and beast were harsh.

Although this is a short hike, be sure to bring water. It's a dehydrating experience.

Miles and Directions

0.0 Follow the asphalt loop trail west of the parking area.

0.2 A use trail leads south from the asphalt path to the hilltop.

0.5 The loop ends right back where you started. The use trail extends out into the salt flats.

1.0 Arrive back at the parking area.

Options: At 0.2 mile a 0.5-mile side trip takes you to a low overlook. Follow the asphalt path that intersects with the loop to the hilltop, which gives you an excellent vista of the central valley floor. From here it is easy to imagine the usual workday in operation here at the Harmony Works. To the east of the hilltop is an area that appears to have been a dump for Furnace Creek. A rusty antique car rests on the hillside, surrounded by desert.

For the 5-mile out and back to the salt flats, the trailhead is located at the far side of Harmony Borax Works, heading west from the loop trail. This hike likewise confirms the arduous conditions of life and work on the valley floor. An unsigned but well-trod path leads west from the end of the paved loop. It travels by a damp slough where groundwater is percolating to the surface, causing borate crystals to form. Farther out on the flats, mounds of borax mud remain where the laborers made piles to validate the works' mining claim more than a hundred years ago.

12 Upper Hole-in-the-Wall

This interesting cross-country canyon trek has lots to see, from marine fossils to grand mountain vistas. Short canyon narrows, geologic wonders, plant species found only in Death Valley, and moderate bouldering add variety to this long loop in the Funeral Mountains.

See map on page 42.
Start: About 12 miles southeast of Furnace Creek.
Distance: 11-mile lollipop.
Approximate hiking time: 6 to 8 hours.
Difficulty: Strenuous.
Trail surface: No trail but sandy gravelly washes and ridges.

Seasons: Mid-October through mid-April.
USGS topo maps: Echo Canyon-CA and East of Echo Canyon-CA (1:24,000).
Trail contact: Furnace Creek Visitor Center & Museum (see appendix D).

Finding the trailhead: From the junction of California Highway 190 and Badwater Road (California Highway 178) south of Furnace Creek, go southeast on CA 190 for 5.4 miles to the Hole-in-the-Wall dirt road on the left. The road is in the wash, near a sign recommending four-wheel-drive vehicles. The first 3.6 miles of the road is rough and rocky, but is often passable by passenger vehicles with slow, careful driving. Drive 3.6 miles to the Hole-in-the-Wall narrows (Split Canyon) and park there, unless you have a high-clearance four-wheel-drive vehicle. If so, you can drive another 2.5 miles to the end of the road just before the wilderness boundary.

Hiking up out of the narrows of the east canyon ▶
in the Red Amphitheater.

The Hike

At the trailhead you'll find remnants of an old travertine quarry. There is another quarry just over the ridge to the north in a small canyon of red sandstone. The quarries produced building stone for the Furnace Creek Inn. From the parking area, hike east for about 0.4-mile to the end of the travertine ridge on the left. You might find pictographs in this area. At this point the basin becomes wider and seems strangely remote, despite its proximity to busy Furnace Creek. Plants of this Mojave Desert ecosystem include creosote, rabbitbrush, barrel cacti, and sweetbush favored by bighorn sheep. At 1 mile you'll see a distinctive black rock outcropping on the left. Across to the south a side drainage leads up to an inner basin on the northeast side of Pyramid Peak. Scan the southern skyline for an arch. Schwaub Peak rises to the northeast, uplifted and tilted with almost vertical sedimentary bedding.

At 1.5 mile turn right (east) up a narrow canyon. Its easier to find the correct canyon if you stay on the right side of the broad valley, which is called Red Amphitheater. A sharp pointed peak marks the right entrance of the canyon. At 2.4 miles the canyon is bounded by dark limestone with moderate bouldering. Look for embedded marine fossils in the limestone. You'll pass through a canyon narrows with cliff walls marked with eroded ripples. These sedimentary rocks were probably mudstone from the floor of an ancient lake bed.

In the next set of narrows we spotted a perfectly camouflaged horned lizard. This is an uncommon reptile, so it pays to be observant. Death Valley goldeneye and napkinring buckwheat grow together in the wash. This secluded rugged terrain is heaven for desert bighorn. As you continue up the canyon, you'll see delicate little ferns clinging to rock walls, and you'll wonder how they can survive in this harsh, dry environment.

At 4 miles an arch sits atop tilted cliffs with eroded pockets used by nesting owls. Just beyond is an obvious gap on the left that leads to the next canyon north. At mile 4.8 a major side gully joins the main east canyon from the right. Continue left for another 0.4 mile and look for a route to the left that crosses the ridge to the next canyon north.

After cresting this divide you might spot another arch to the west as you descend to the north canyon. You might also see a light lavender flower with a yellow center known as rock nimulus growing from limestone cracks—these are endemic to Death Valley.

Upon reaching the main canyon floor at around 5.7 miles, turn left (west) and hike down the wash for the return leg of the loop. This stretch contains such wonders as beehive cacti, Death Valley penstemon, marine fossils, and great towering spires and cliffs. Try to avoid rock nettles or you'll learn the hard way why they're called "velcro" plants. The canyon walls are made of hard, sandy conglomerate, riddled with openings and alcoves. At 7.3 miles the canyon opens, with enticing side canyons to the right that invite further exploration.

When the limestone ridge on the left ends at about mile 8.2, you'll be looking straight south to the Black Mountains. The loop is completed at 9.5 miles. Continue down to the trailhead to finish this varied 11-mile canyon route in Death Valley's Funeral Mountains.

Miles and Directions

0.0 Begin at the trailhead/wilderness boundary.

0.4 Reach the end of the travertine ridge.

1.5 Enter the side canyon to the right (east).

3.2 With the low saddle on the left, continue to the right up the main wash.

4.2 This is the crossover point for the shorter loop option.

5.2 Climb the ridge to the left (north).

5.7 At the north canyon, turn left for the downhill (return) leg of the loop.

9.5 Complete the basic loop near the canyon junction.

11.0 Return to the trailhead.

Options: The loop can be shortened by 2 or 3 miles by crossing north to the next canyon at about mile 4.2. You can identify the spot by the color of the rocks: red on the left, white to the right, and black limestone straight ahead.

From the upper crossover ridge described in the hike, and before dropping to the next canyon north, climb up the steep ridge to the right (east) for expansive views of Amargosa Valley far into Nevada.

From the Hole-in-the-Wall narrows, 3.6 road miles above CA 190, a short 2-mile round-trip provides desert panoramas, majestic rock formations, and varied terrain. The hike begins at the Hole-in-the-Wall cliffs of differentially eroded volcanic ash. The narrows are also known as Split Canyon. The multitude of holes form enchanting shapes; some are precise, while others droop. To the north, beyond the alluvial fan, lie the Funeral Mountains. Travel north-northwest using the varnished desert pavement where possible since the wash winds a bit and is loaded with boulders that make hiking difficult. You gain 420 feet in elevation by the time you reach the canyon mouth. Here more towering limestone cliffs display the eyes and mouths of erosion holes. The canyon floor is a wide graveled wash. The canyon narrows and turns at 0.3 mile, only to be blocked by a 40-foot dry fall. The tempting sidehill to the west is too unstable and dangerous for climbing, so this is the terminal point of the canyon hike. At the canyon mouth, hike east 0.2 mile to the next canyon. This one is totally blocked by massive boulders. The return descent to Hole-in-the-Wall features magnificent views of the Artist's Drive Formation at the northern end of the Black Mountains, with Death Valley stretching out beyond. Telescope Peak stands on the far horizon.

13 Keane Wonder Mine

An old mining road in the Funeral Mountains leads to the historic ruins of mines, a mill, and tramways. The route is steep and rocky, and the scenic views down the canyon to Death Valley are dramatic.

Start: About 20 miles north of Furnace Creek.
Distance: 4 miles out and back.
Approximate hiking time: 2 to 3 hours.
Difficulty: Strenuous.
Trail surface: Rocky trail.

Seasons: October through April.
USGS topo map: Chloride City-CA (1:24,000).
Trail contact: Furnace Creek Visitor Center & Museum (see appendix D).

Finding the trailhead: From Nevada Highway 374/Daylight Pass Road at Hell's Gate Junction, head south on Beatty Cutoff Road going toward Beatty Junction. After 4.3 miles turn left on the signed Keane Wonder Mine Road, a good gravel route, and drive 2.8 miles east to the end-of-the-road parking area below the Keane Wonder Mill.

From the visitor center at Furnace Creek, drive north on California Highway 190 for 11.3 miles to Beatty Cutoff Road and continue right (north) on Beatty-Daylight Pass Cutoff Road for another 5.7 miles to Keane Wonder Mine Road. Turn right and drive the final 2.8 miles to the end-of-the-road parking area/trailhead.

The Hike

The Keane Wonder Mine was developed at a time and in a location of hundreds of gold, silver, and lead strikes. The relative success of this venture makes its history and today's ruins all the more intriguing. It all began in 1903 with an almost-unheard-of lucky strike by an unemployed Irish miner named Jack Keane and his partner. After months of futile searching for silver, Keane accidentally stumbled across a huge ledge of gold, calling the find the "Keane Wonder Mine" out of his total astonishment at being so fortunate.

The news spread rapidly, and by 1904 the local gold rush was on. The mine changed hands several times, making a fortune for its original partners, and was capitalized with stocks sold to an eager public. In 1906 Homer Wilson bought the mine and started a consortium that operated the mine for a decade. Wilson ordered a twenty-stamp mill to crush the ore and a gravity-operated aerial tramway nearly 1 mile long. Loaded ore buckets coming down the canyon from the shaft pulled the empty buckets back up. The tram contained thirteen towers, with the longest span being 1,200 feet, and a vertical drop from top to bottom of 1,500 feet. Lack of water prevented the mill from operating at full capacity. Even so, total gold production from the mine was around $1.1 million, most of which was extracted between 1907 and 1911.

The Keane Wonder Mine aerial tramway terminal overlooks a steep rugged canyon.

The Keane Wonder Mine was one of the two largest producing gold mines in the Death Valley region, the other being the Skidoo Mine. The artifacts and remnants of this mine have significant historical value and should not be removed or disturbed in any way.

From the parking area, climb 0.1 mile to the informative kiosk located just below the Keane Wonder Mill ruins. The sign contains a bit of the history of Jack Keane's amazing 1903 gold strike. From the trailhead, extensive mining debris can be seen in the wash to the left. At 0.4 mile the trail crosses under the tramway and begins a very steep climb straight up the ridge. In just 0.7 mile another 650 feet elevation is gained, at which point the trail contours and climbs more moderately to the right above the tramway canyon leading to the mine. At 1.7 miles the trail reaches the large aerial tramway terminal structure along with several shallow mine shafts.

From here a level trail extends another 0.5 mile around the canyon to an upper mine area containing additional adits. The view down canyon makes this short extension of the hike more than worthwhile. Another narrow trail climbs steeply 0.2

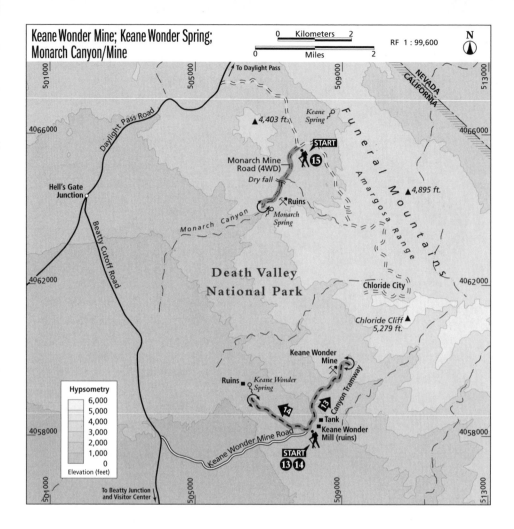

mile to the base of the main mine, which peers from the steep mountainside at around 3,000 feet elevation. Several stone building foundations are passed along the way. Around the bend and at the base of the mine, the area beyond is closed to hiking for public safety. Unsecured mine shafts present hazards and should definitely be avoided. Enjoy them from a safe distance before retracing your route to the trailhead, as you complete this round-trip hiking climb to one of Death Valley's largest and most interesting early-twentieth-century mining ventures.

Miles and Directions

0.0   Start at the trailhead/parking area.

0.1   Stop at the kiosk below the Keane Wonder Mill ruins.

1.7   Arrive at the aerial tramway terminal.

2.0   View the stone building foundations and mine shafts below the main mine openings.

4.0   Return to the trailhead.

14 Keane Wonder Spring

This nearly level trip takes you to the spring that was essential to the Keane Wonder Mine and mill operations. The area has many traces of mining activities of the last century.

See map on page 56.
Start: About 20 miles north of Furnace Creek.
Length: 2 miles out and back.
Approximate hiking time: 1 to 2 hours.
Difficulty: Easy.
Trail surface: Sandy, rocky path.

Seasons: October through April.
USGS topo map: Chloride City-CA (1:24,000).
Trail contact: Furnace Creek Visitor Center & Museum (see appendix D).

Finding the trailhead: From Nevada Highway 374, 19.3 miles southwest of Beatty, Nevada, turn left (south) on Beatty Cutoff Road and drive 4.3 miles to the signed dirt road on your left. Take the gravel road 2.8 miles to the Keane Wonder Mine parking area.

From Furnace Creek, go north on California Highway 190 11.3 miles north of the visitor center. Turn right (east) on the Beatty Cutoff and drive 5.7 miles to the Keane Wonder gravel road on your right. Drive 2.8 miles to the Keane Wonder Mine parking area. The trail to the spring begins at the northeastern corner of the parking area and heads north.

The Hike

The Keane Wonder Mine complex was at its height in the gold boom from 1906 to 1912. It was resuscitated by optimistic prospectors and investors several times. The most recent renaissance was in 1935–37 when cyanide leaching of the mine tailings took place on the site. The tanks used for that operation stand below the parking area.

Where the mine trail goes directly up the hillside, the use trail to Keane Wonder Spring goes left. The trail begins after you drop into the debris-strewn wash just north of the parking area. Emerging from the wash above the pair of settling tanks nestled together, you pick up the well-traveled trail. A broken pipeline lies 50 yards below on the hillside; it will lead you to the springs.

The trail travels by numerous mine openings and scenic travertine rock outcroppings. At 0.6 mile the trail merges with the trail coming up from lower on the hillside; you'll return to the parking area via this trail on the hike back. More mine openings and a stone foundation are nearby. The trail is meticulously bordered with rocks for most of the way.

Continuing northward, soon your nose will detect the scent of sulfur, even on a windy day. There, at 0.8 mile, the trickling stream from the spring crosses the road. Above the trail take a side trip to the spring. The salt grass marsh flourishes in the salt-encrusted soil 30 yards above the trail. A sign posted by the National Park Service warns of gas hazards in the mine shaft immediately above the spring. The area has many mine shafts, some flooded, all dangerous.

Salt grass thrives in the marsh at Keane Wonder Spring.

This mining wasteland is also full of wildlife. Heavy bighorn-sheep use is evident from the droppings on the damp spring banks. Birds and crickets create a symphony of sound in the desert stillness.

Continuing northward, the trail follows a crude aqueduct and curves around, now totally out of sight of the parking area and industrial sprawl there. More of the ubiquitous mine sites and another sulfurous spring bracket the trail. At your destination, 1 mile, you'll find a mine chute and a miner's cabin. Rusty cans, pieces of pipe, and the usual pieces of nondescript rusty artifacts litter the ground. In the dry desert air, the cabin is so well preserved it appears the miner left recently. Across the shallow gully to the west is a large rock outcropping atop a hill. Notice the stone walls built under the natural overhang. Did wind, heat, or both drive the miner to take refuge in such a primitive rock shelter?

Return the way you came, continuing on the wide rock-lined trail at the junction you passed on the way in. In sight of the parking area, the trail dissipates in the mine debris in the gully near the largest of the remaining tanks. From there you have to pick your way back to your vehicle.

The amazing thing about the Keane Wonder Spring hike is its plethora of mine sites. The Keane Wonder Mine was heralded to be the richest gold strike in Death Valley, attracting a multitude of hopeful miners. At its height nearly 500 prospectors were working in the area. Thus, everywhere you look, there's another mine mouth with its tailings dripping down the hillside. Mine tunnels like rabbit holes cut through the ridges and disappear into mountainside. Curious children and adults should avoid all mines.

Miles and Directions

0.0 The trail heads north above the pair of settling tanks.

0.3 The trail crosses a wash and continues following the contour of the hillside.

0.6 The trail merges with another trail from the lower hillside. Continue on the trail to the spring/mine site.

0.8 The first spring crosses the trail. An aqueduct ditch parallels the trail.

1.0 Arrive at a mine chute and cabin and another sulfur seep.

2.0 Return to the trailhead.

15 Monarch Canyon/Mine

This out-and-back hike takes you down a rocky canyon in the Funeral Mountains to an 80-foot dry fall, a well-preserved stamp mill, and a desert spring.

See map on page 56.
Start: About 27.5 miles north of Furnace Creek.
Distance: 3 miles out and back.
Approximate hiking time: 2 to 3 hours.
Difficulty: Easy.

Trail surface: Four-wheel-drive road, rocky trail, clear wash.
Seasons: October through April.
USGS topo map: Chloride City-CA (1:24,000).
Trail contact: Furnace Creek Visitor Center & Museum (see appendix D).

Finding the trailhead: From Nevada Highway 374/Daylight Pass Road 3.4 miles northeast of Hell's Gate Junction in Boundary Canyon and 15.8 miles southwest of Beatty, Nevada, look for a road to the south that is marked only with a small sign recommending four-wheel drive. Carefully driven high-clearance two-wheel-drive vehicles can negotiate this road for 2.2 miles to the bottom of upper Monarch Canyon. High-clearance four-wheel drive is required for vehicular travel beyond this point to Chloride City. The rough Monarch Mine Road takes off south from this point. This road junction can serve as the trailhead for the hike down Monarch Canyon. However, the hike can be shortened by 1.2 miles round-trip by driving down Monarch Mine Road to a point just above the dry fall.

The Hike

Hikers can start at the unsigned junction between the rough Chloride City Road and four-wheel-drive Monarch Mine Road (3 miles round-trip to Monarch Spring) or at the end of the Monarch Mine Road (1.8 miles round-trip). From the Chloride City Road junction, the trip starts out in rounded, low-lying hills. The four-wheel-drive road descends southwesterly, entering a rocky canyon after 0.3 mile.

At 0.6 mile the road ends above a striking 80-foot dry fall. A major side canyon enters from the left, bounded by high cliffs marked by folded multicolored bands of rock. Continue left around the falls on the old mining trail. After another 0.1 mile the trail drops to the wash, which is covered with horsetails and Mormon tea. This is favored habitat for quail and other birds. The base of the dry falls is definitely worth visiting, so turn right and walk 0.1 mile up to the precipice. In addition to the main wide falls, another smaller but equally high falls guards the canyon bowl to the left. The canyon walls are distinguished by shelf rock catch basins, overhangs, and contorted layers of colorful, twisted rock.

Proceeding back down the sandy canyon wash, an eroded-out mining trail crosses to the right and then drops back to the canyon floor at 1 mile. Rock cairns are in place for the return trip. At 1.2 miles the wood and cement ruins of the Monarch Mine stamp mill are reached on the left. The ore chute to the mill extends up an almost vertical rock face.

To further experience the rugged grandeur of Monarch Canyon, continue down the wash another 0.3 mile to the brushy bottom just below Monarch Spring. Here the canyon bends sharply to the right and begins to narrow. Hiking below the spring would be difficult due to dense vegetation and loose, rocky side slopes. Retrace your route.

Miles and Directions

0.0 Start at the trailhead at the junction of Chloride City Road and Monarch Mine Road in upper Monarch Canyon.

0.6 Arrive at an 80-foot dry fall at the end of Monarch Mine Road.

0.7 The mining trail drops to the bottom of a canyon wash.

0.8 Walk up the wash to the base of the dry falls.

1.2 Arrive at the Monarch Mine stamp mill ruins.

1.5 Arrive at Monarch Spring.

3.0 Return to the trailhead by the same route.

◀ *The base of the Monarch Mine stamp mill.*

16 Hungry Bill's Ranch/Johnson Canyon

This out-and-back hike follows a scenic stream up a canyon to the historic ruins of Bill's 1870s ranch deep in the Panamint Mountains.

Start: About 37 miles southwest of Furnace Creek.
Distance: 3.8 miles out and back.
Approximate hiking time: 3 to 4 hours.
Difficulty: Strenuous.

Trail surface: Primitive use trail.
Seasons: October through May.
USGS topo map: Panamint-CA (1:24,000).
Trail contact: Furnace Creek Visitor Center & Museum (see appendix D).

Finding the trailhead: From California Highway 190 at the Furnace Creek Inn, drive south on Badwater Road (California Highway 178) for 7.1 miles; turn to the southwest on the washboard/gravel West Side Road (closed during summer) and continue south for another 21.7 miles to Johnson Canyon Road; turn right (west) and drive 9.7 miles to a point about 0.1 mile before the end of the road at Wilson Spring. It is best to park about 0.1 mile below Wilson Spring to avoid driving through the riparian area and thick brush. The final 3.4 miles to the trailhead require a high-clearance four-wheel-drive vehicle. Those with standard two-wheel-drive vehicles should park at or near the burro pen before the rough road drops steeply into the canyon. This will add about 7 miles round-trip distance to the hike. The primitive use trail begins at Wilson Spring, following the stream drainage 1.8 miles to the upper ranch site.

The Hike

The original Hungry Bill's Ranch in upper Johnson Canyon was first developed in the 1870s by Swiss farmers who sought to grow fruits and vegetables for sale to the residents of Panamint City, over rugged Panamint Pass in Surprise Canyon. The mining camp had its brief heyday from 1874 to 1877. By the time the Swiss farmers were ready to sell their produce, bust had followed boom and the market had vanished! Later the ranch was occupied for many years by a Shoshone Indian named Hungry Bill, whose huge appetite matched his great girth. Today all that remains are fruit trees and extensive stone walls.

The road up Johnson Canyon is very rough, requiring high-clearance four-wheel drive in order to reach the road-end trailhead at Wilson Spring. Wilson Spring is a lush and lovely spot with water pouring from a pipe, huge willow and cottonwood trees, and an informal campsite—a true desert oasis. In the absence of four-wheel drive, plan on parking at the burro pen about 3.5 miles short of Wilson Spring, thereby adding 7 miles round-trip to the hike.

The South Fork of Johnson Canyon enters from the left 1 mile before reaching Wilson Spring. This canyon is wide and graveled and can be hiked up toward the crest of the Panamint Mountains as a side trip.

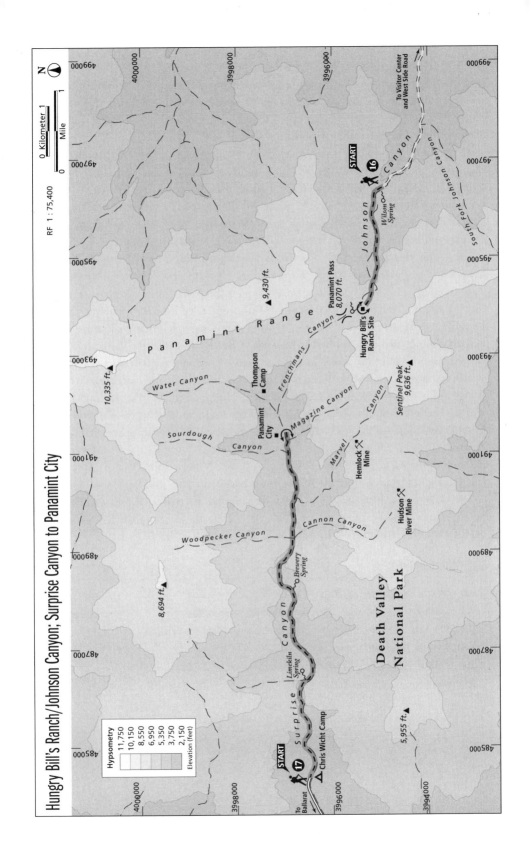

Hungry Bill's Ranch/Johnson Canyon; Surprise Canyon to Panamint City

RF 1 : 75,400

N

0 Kilometer 1

0 Mile 1

Hypsometry

11,750
10,150
8,550
6,950
5,350
3,750
2,150

Elevation (feet)

Panamint Range

10,335 ft. ▲

9,430 ft. ▲

Water Canyon

Sourdough Canyon

Thompson Camp ■

Panamint City ■

Frenchmans Canyon

Magazine Canyon

Panamint Pass 8,070 ft.

Hungry Bill's Ranch Site

Wilson Spring

START 16

Johnson Canyon

To Visitor Center and West Side Road

South Fork Johnson Canyon

Marvel Canyon

Sentinel Peak 9,636 ft. ▲

Hemlock Mine ✗

Hudson River Mine ✗

Cannon Canyon

Woodpecker Canyon

8,694 ft. ▲

Brewery Spring

Surprise Canyon

Limekiln Spring

Chris Wicht Camp ▲

START 17

To Ballarat

5,955 ft. ▲

Death Valley National Park

4000000
3998000
3396000

499000
497000
495000
493000
491000
489000
487000
485000

To reach Hungry Bill's Ranch from just below Wilson Spring, look for the use trail that heads up the canyon on the left side from the road end. Within 0.2 mile the trail passes the circular stone remnants of an arrastra used by miners for crushing ore. At 0.3 mile the trail fades out. Cross the canyon wash to the right side and look carefully for the continuation of the trail.

At 0.4 mile the canyon narrows, bounded by high rugged cliffs of volcanic rhyolite rock. The primitive trail crosses back and forth through the wash. The canyon again narrows at 0.6 mile; cross and climb around rock spires to the left. At 0.7 mile the trail climbs past hand-built rock walls and then loses 100 feet as it drops to the stream bottom. With a profusion of birds, frogs, lush vegetation, and water, this delightful stretch of Johnson Canyon is a refreshing celebration of life!

At 1 mile the trail reaches an overlook after contouring up and down along the steep rocky slopes. The trail then drops another 50 feet to the stream, crosses to the right, then the left, and continues up canyon to the lower ranch site on the right (north) side at 1.6 miles. Each stream crossing features well-placed stepping stones, so you are guaranteed a dry journey. At the lower ranch, the rock walls, fruit trees, and gurgling rivulet are overseen by massive cliffs toward Panamint Pass.

Cross to the left side and follow the primitive trail another 0.1 mile, where the stream has disappeared beneath the ground—a completely different and drier world. At 1.9 miles the stream resurfaces at the main Hungry Bill's Ranch—a huge open area on the left (south) side of the canyon. The site includes fruit trees surrounded by extensive rock walls. A rock-walled roofless house protected by a stone wall windbreak sits on a hill above the ranch. Hungry Bill certainly had a stunning view of an incredibly rugged cliff face, and down across Death Valley to the Black Mountains. It is interesting to reflect on the life he must have led.

You'll probably have an easier time following the use trail back down to Wilson Spring than you did on the way up. With the scenic canyon, rough trail, and ample exploration opportunities at the ranch, there is no need to hurry.

Miles and Directions

0.0 Start at the trailhead, located 0.1 mile below Wilson Spring.

0.3 Where the use trail fades, cross the canyon to the right side.

0.6 The canyon narrows. Cross and climb around the rock spires to the left.

1.6 Arrive at Hungry Bill's lower ranch.

1.9 Arrive at Hungry Bill's Ranch. After exploring, return by the same route.

3.8 Arrive back at the trailhead.

A bubbling brook flows down Johnson Canyon at 1 mile. ▶

17 Surprise Canyon to Panamint City

The hike to the ghost town of Panamint City follows a year-round canyon stream through a lengthy, dramatic canyon. Contemporary mining activity mingles with the historic in this remote Panamint Mountain location.

See map on page 63.
Start: About 65 miles south of Stovepipe Wells Village.
Length: 13 miles out and back.
Approximate hiking time: 4 to 7 hours.
Difficulty: Strenuous.

Trail surface: Rocky path.
Seasons: September through May.
USGS topo maps: Ballarat-CA and Panamint-CA (1:24,000).
Trail contact: Furnace Creek Visitor Center & Museum (see appendix D).

Finding the trailhead: From California Highway 190, 34.5 miles southwest of Stovepipe Wells and 2.6 miles east of Panamint Springs Resort, go south on Panamint Valley Road for 13.9 miles to the junction with Trona-Wildrose Road. Turn right (south) and drive 9.5 miles to Ballarat Road (signed) on your left. Turn left and go 3.6 miles to the tiny town of Ballarat. Turn left at the general store, which is a good stop for ice, cold sodas, and lively conversation with the proprietor. From the store, drive north on Indian Ranch Road 1.9 miles to Surprise Canyon Road on your right, which is marked by a signpost and by a large white boulder with a red S7 on it. Turn right and drive 4.1 miles to the road's end at the Chris Wicht Camp. Park on the side and speak to the occupant if he is around. Do not block the road or the driveway. Be considerate of those living here.

The Hike

The Surprise Canyon hike is located on the very western edge of the expansion area of Death Valley National Park above the Panamint Valley. The BLM Surprise Canyon Wilderness Area lies on both sides of Surprise Canyon Road off Indian Canyon Road. Here the BLM's open desert camping regulations are in effect; there are plentiful campsites along the first 2 miles of Surprise Canyon Road before it climbs the alluvial fan.

The Wicht Camp on the topo map straddles the end of the driveable road. The Novaks are living here. Please show respect and do not disturb the residents. The Novaks will keep an eye on your vehicle for the price of a six-pack. Don't, however, poke around their dwelling; there will be plenty to explore in Panamint City, 6.5 miles and 3,000 feet higher ahead.

A practical piece of advice is to waterproof your boots before hiking here—especially if the springs are running at full capacity. The trail/river combination makes for very damp hiking in the lower 3.5 miles of the canyon. This is a minor inconvenience in this adventuresome climb to Panamint City.

A mine mill site in Surprise Canyon just above the trailhead.

The vegetation and wildlife of Surprise Canyon is varied and plentiful, due to the presence of water and the elevation change. Birds and burros frequent the lower canyon. The hike will travel through several vegetative zones as it climbs, from the riparian willow groves to creosote scrub community to piñon-juniper forest. From your destination in Panamint City, the lofty cliffs of the mountain range soar above forested slopes.

Right from the start the hike up Surprise Canyon is a startling change from the drive through Panamint Valley. Even the bumpy ride up the road to the parking area does not hint at the water and greenery that greet you at Wicht Camp. The first 0.5 mile from the camp involves repeated zigzags along the shallow stream to dry sections of the largely washed-out trail. To enjoy the views of the rugged canyon walls, it is necessary to pause between stream leaps.

At 1 mile, hand and foot scrambling is necessary to get up the sloping gorge, where wet rocks are quite slippery. Another more challenging gorge lies 0.2 mile beyond, leading up to a broader valley. An amusing sight above the gorge is the deserted mine vehicle perched in the eroded trail. More vehicles lie in the brush, probably brought down the valley by the 1984 flood. During this lower third of the hike to Panamint City the watery trail periodically becomes dry, but the flow from Limekiln and Brewery Springs along the canyon revives the creek.

At 3.4 miles the damp trail bisects an arched willow grove and cuts by a rocky grotto. This is the last contact with the stream until the return trip. The next mile and a half of the hike climbs 1,000 feet, with rugged canyon walls of contrasting colors on both sides. Juniper, Mormon tea, and barrel cacti crowd the lower slopes, with barren cliffs bursting above.

By 5 miles you'll begin to spot remains of Panamint City's vast mining activities. Up to 2,000 people lived in the narrow city during its brief heyday in the mid-1870 silver boom. Even today validated mining claims exist here.

At 6.2 miles you'll arrive at the central city site, where it is evident that mining and residential activities have occurred recently. Several cabins are located in the valley above the smelter ruins. Respect private property during your visit. The interface of old and modern mining is also in evidence. Aluminum and plastic debris from the 1950s is mixed with the more traditional rusty tin cans and barrel hoops of ghost towns. Amazingly, much industrial equipment is located in this hard-to-reach spot: a 20-foot propane tank, two trailers, various trucks, and other heavy machinery. Some 1950s-vintage buildings are interspersed with remains of the last century's occupation.

The narrow valley floor below the modern mining outpost is overgrown with creosote and catclaw. Amid the shrubbery are the stone walls and foundations of the nineteenth-century dwellers. Near one of the larger building sites a garden of iris continues to spring merrily into life, a living artifact of Panamint City's brief but optimistic history. A large stone-walled livestock paddock remains on the north side of the trail; it is apparent that the wild burros of the canyon still like to hang out here.

Binoculars will enable you to explore the canyon visually without plowing through the dense vicious shrubs. Several other canyons branch out at the eastern end of Surprise Canyon. With topo map in hand, you can explore Frenchmans Canyon to the southeast toward Panamint Pass, or Water Canyon to the northeast. Thompson Camp, in the latter, is 0.5 mile beyond the upper end of Panamint City by way of an aqueduct trail. A couple of wooden-shell buildings and a water tank mark its 6,500-foot location. There is also a lush spring (Thompson Spring), with a large wooden cask cistern that used to supply the mining community. It is an excellent source of water even today.

Above the industrial city rise the peaks of the Panamints. The towering wall of the divide rises sharply 3,000 feet above the town, dwarfing the 100-foot chimney of the deteriorating smelter. The miners have come and gone, but the majesty of this desert mountain range persists.

Miles and Directions

0.0 Hike up the former road by Novak Mill. Do not linger near the mill site: The Novak family is wary of intruders.

0.1–0.5 The trail and river share the same bed, necessitating much stream-hopping.

2.8 At the junction with the canyon from the south, continue on the trail (left) up the main canyon.

3.5 This is the last willow grove—your feet will stay dry from here on.

4.9 Arrive at a mine opening on the right.

5.0 At this major canyon junction, Woodpecker enters from the north, Cannon from the south; continue straight up the main Surprise Canyon.

5.4 Marvel Canyon joins from the south at the trail junction. There's a low rock wall on the left. The chimney of the Panamint City smelter is visible a mile ahead.

6.2 Arrive at the junction with Sourdough Canyon from the north.

6.5 View the smelter ruins. The roads branch off to various other mine sites in Magazine, Water, and Frenchmans Canyons. This is the turnaround point for the hike back to the trailhead.

13.0 Return to the trailhead.

18 Telescope Peak

The trek to Telescope Peak is a strenuous all-day hike to the highest point in the park. From here you have spectacular vistas made even more impressive given the astounding elevation difference of 11,300 feet from the valley below.

Start: About 40 miles south of Stovepipe Wells Village.
Distance: 14 miles out and back.
Approximate hiking time: 7 to 10 hours.
Difficulty: Strenuous.
Trail surface: Dirt path with some rocky areas.

Seasons: Mid-May to mid-November. Check at the ranger station for weather information affecting the Wildrose Canyon Road.
USGS topo map: Telescope Peak-CA (1:24,000).
Trail contact: Furnace Creek Visitor Center & Museum (see appendix D).

Finding the trailhead: The trail begins at the south end of the Mahogany Flat Campground at the end of upper Mahogany Flat Road 8.7 miles east of Wildrose Junction. To reach the trailhead, take Emigrant Canyon Road 20.9 miles south of California Highway 190 to Wildrose Junction. Continue on Mahogany Flat Road. The upper section of the road is rough and steep for the final 1.6 miles after the charcoal kilns.

During winter Mahogany Flat Road above the charcoal kilns is often blocked by snow, adding 3.2 miles to the already long round-trip distance to Telescope Peak. If you are unable to drive all the way to the campground, start the hike from the Thorndike Campground (7.8 miles east of Wildrose Junction) or from the Charcoal Kilns parking area (7.1 miles east of Wildrose Junction). This will add 0.9 mile or 1.6 miles, respectively, to the hike each way, making an early start imperative.

The Hike

The 7-mile trail to the top of Telescope Peak is one of only two constructed backcountry trails in all of Death Valley National Park. Although no rock cairns or tree blazes mark the way, the clear trail is easy to follow throughout its length. After the snow melts by mid- to late spring, there is no water anywhere along the high, dry ridge route, so be sure to carry an ample supply.

An average 8 percent grade is maintained, but there are long stretches where no significant elevation is gained or lost as well as several very steep switchback pitches to the summit. This high-ridge trail hike is especially enjoyable during summer when temperatures are usually unbearable in the valleys on both sides of Telescope Peak—11,000 feet below. This lofty stretch of the Panamint Mountains catches and holds a lot of snow during winter, but the peak can sometimes be climbed without difficulty as early as mid-March with only a mile or so of deep ridgeline snow to "posthole" up just before reaching the summit. During winter it may be easier and safer to avoid the first 2 miles of steep sidehill trail by proceeding straight up the ridge over Rogers Peak. Winter climbers should register at the Wildrose Ranger

The 11,049-foot Telescope Peak rises to the south.

Station before and after the climb, and carry and know how to use ice axes, crampons, and winter clothing.

Backcountry camping is allowed 2 miles beyond the trailhead, but the first level and somewhat protected tent site is 2.6 miles in, along the edge of Arcane Meadows.

From the signed trailhead, the trail starts in a forest of large, old piñon and limber pines, thinning gradually as the elevation increases. A trail register is positioned at 0.2 mile. The trail climbs moderately for 2 miles with spectacular views into the rugged North Fork Hanaupah Canyon, which drains eastward to Death Valley. At 2.6 miles the broad plateau of Arcane Meadows is reached at an elevation of 9,620 feet. This high sagebrush saddle is on the north summit ridge of Telescope Peak, directly below and southwest of the communications facility on Rogers Peak. Twisted tree trunks add a distinctive foreground to the sweep of the high Sierras far to the west, with the wide Tuber Canyon dropping steeply at first and then more gradually into a broad valley.

At 2.7 miles the trail leaves Arcane Meadows as it wraps around the west- to northwest-facing slopes of 9,980-foot Bennett Peak. Expect that about 0.5 mile of this stretch of trail will be snow-covered into early May.

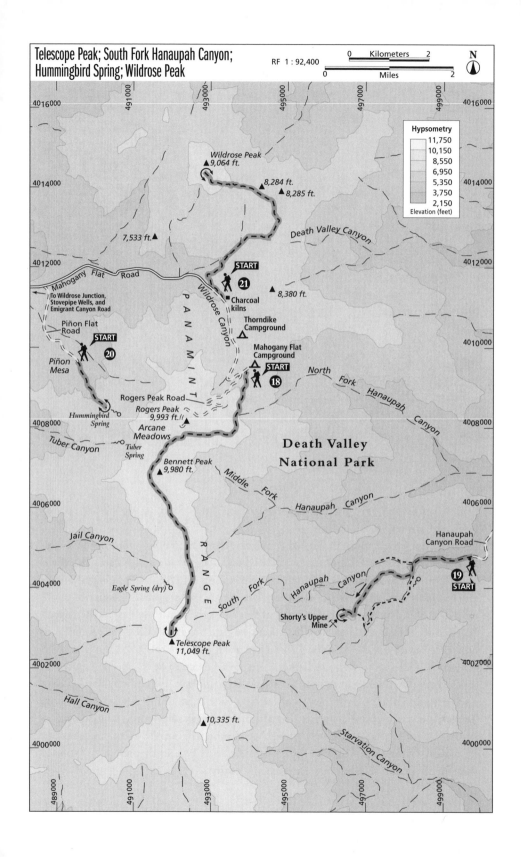

Telescope Peak; South Fork Hanaupah Canyon; Hummingbird Spring; Wildrose Peak

RF 1 : 92,400

Kilometers 0 — 2

Miles 0 — 2

N

Hypsometry

11,750
10,150
8,550
6,950
5,350
3,750
2,150

Elevation (feet)

Wildrose Peak
▲9,064 ft.

8,284 ft.
▲ 8,285 ft.

7,533 ft.▲

Death Valley Canyon

START 21

■ Charcoal kilns

▲ 8,380 ft.

Mahogany Flat Road

← To Wildrose Junction, Stovepipe Wells, and Emigrant Canyon Road

Piñon Flat Road

START 20

Piñon Mesa

Hummingbird Spring

Thorndike Campground

Mahogany Flat Campground

START 18

North Fork Hanaupah Canyon

P A N A M I N T

Wildrose Canyon

Rogers Peak Road

Rogers Peak 9,993 ft.▲

Arcane Meadows

Tuber Canyon

Tuber Spring

Bennett Peak ▲9,980 ft.

Middle Fork Hanaupah Canyon

Death Valley National Park

Jail Canyon

R A N G E

Eagle Spring (dry) ○

South Fork Hanaupah Canyon

Shorty's Upper Mine ✕

Hanaupah Canyon Road

19 **START**

▲Telescope Peak 11,049 ft.

Hall Canyon

▲10,335 ft.

Starvation Canyon

At 4.3 miles the trail reaches the 9,500-foot saddle south of Bennett Peak. In another 0.2 mile the nearly level trail intersects an unsigned side trail, which takes off to the right, climbing first then dropping 1 mile to dry Eagle Spring. Talus rock mixed with matted low-lying vegetation and prickly pear cacti add an unusual alpine tundra/high desert flavor. At the junction follow the trail to the left around the east side of the mountain and then back up to the summit ridge at 5 miles.

After another 0.5 mile the trail reaches the south upper end of the rugged cliffs of Jail Canyon at 9,970 feet. Huge bristlecone pine snags provide irresistible photo opportunities. The trail begins a series of steep switchbacks just right (east) of the sharp summit ridge, attaining an elevation of 10,400 feet at 6.2 miles. Gigantic gnarled bristlecone pines adorn these higher slopes. Some of these ancient trees have been bored and are around 3,000 years old. Members of the same species in the nearby White Mountains are among the oldest living creatures on earth at some 4,600 years!

The 11,000-foot mark is finally achieved at 6.8 miles. From here the trail climbs three mounds along the ridge before reaching the one farthest south at 7 miles—this is 11,049-foot Telescope Peak. The summit consists of a long rocky point, dropping off steeply to the south, west, and east. Mercifully, the actual peak is often less windy than the exposed ridge going up, so if conditions are tolerable, spend some time reading and signing the peak register.

The vertical relief is amazing, almost impossible to comprehend unless you make it to the top and look down on the salt flats of Badwater—the lowest point in the Western Hemisphere—more than 11,300 feet directly below. This monumental elevation difference is exceeded in the United States by only three other mountains: Mount Rainier in Washington and Mounts McKinley and Fairweather in Alaska. Telescope also affords a grand distant view of the highest point in the continental United States—14,494-foot Mount Whitney.

The vast desert basins of Panamint and Death Valley surround jagged canyons that emanate from Telescope Peak like spokes on a wheel. The remarkable contrast of basins and ranges that seem to stretch to infinity on a 360-degree arc is made even more dramatic when snow mantles the summit and higher ridges. Retrace your route to conclude a long, invigorating day on Death Valley's rooftop.

Miles and Directions

0.0 Start at the trailhead at Mahogany Flat Campground.

2.6 Arrive at Arcane Meadows.

4.3 Arrive at the saddle before the summit ridge to the peak.

7.0 Reach the summit of Telescope Peak.

14.0 Return to the trailhead.

Option: For an enjoyable 4-mile loop, hike to the end of the gated Rogers Peak Road, then up the ridge to intersect the Telescope Peak Trail, then north on the trail back to the Mahogany Flat trailhead.

19 South Fork Hanaupah Canyon

This vigorous hike on the eastern slopes of the Panamint Range includes a diverse canyon with springs, waterfalls, and a permanent stream, along with some of the most spectacular vistas in Death Valley. Other attractions include old mining artifacts and a chance to see wildlife.

See map on page 72.
Start: About 27 miles southwest of Furnace Creek.
Distance: 6 miles out and back from upper trailhead (add 6 or 7 miles if driving a 2-wheel-drive vehicle).
Approximate hiking time: 3 to 4 hours (plus another 3 to 4 hours if optional side canyon route is chosen).

Difficulty: Moderate (strenuous for option).
Trail surface: Old rocky mining road with rough sections of rock talus.
Seasons: Mid-September to mid-May.
USGS topo maps: Hanaupah Canyon-CA and Telescope Peak-CA (1:24,000).
Trail contact: Furnace Creek Visitor Center & Museum (see appendix D).

Finding the trailhead: From State Highway 190, drive 7.1 miles south on Badwater Road (California Highway 178); take West Side Road and drive 10.7 miles south to the rough Hanaupah Canyon Road. Hanaupah Canyon Road is also 25 miles north of the southern Badwater Road/West Side Road junction. Like all of the canyon roads on the east side of the Panamints, this road climbs up a rocky alluvial fan. The first 4.8 miles of this 8.3-mile-long road can be driven with a high-clearance two-wheel-drive vehicle. Then the road drops into the canyon and becomes four-wheel drive to the end. Once there, find a wide spot to park at the unsigned trailhead.

The Hike

Begin by hiking up the brushy bottom of the South Fork of Hanaupah Canyon. Hug the left side of the canyon wall to pick up a use trail next to the stream. The springs that feed Hanaupah Canyon discharge an amazing 250-plus gallons per minute, nurturing a diverse riparian corridor that attracts a wide array of wildlife. The old mines and cabin of "Shorty" Borden are on the hillsides above the springs. The trail cuts through an eroded alluvial fan and reaches permanent water at 0.6 mile, as evidenced by willow thickets. This is also the junction of an old mining road that leads to the upper mine. From here it's about 0.3 mile up the brushy bottom to a waterfall. Many of the granite boulders along the streambed are embedded with feldspar crystals, the same Little Chief granite found on Telescope Peak.

To continue the longer hike to the upper mine, head up the old mining road to the left. The next mile gains 1,000 feet, with breathtaking views of a side canyon waterfall and of Death Valley. The two-track is rough but provides a good hiking

Bouldering down a side canyon south of the
South Fork of Hanaupah Canyon.

trail. It continues climbing up a center ridge between the South Fork of Hanaupah Canyon and an unnamed tributary to the south.

Usually by March the road cuts are ablaze with cliffrose and Indian paintbrush. The trail keeps climbing with some very steep pitches, gaining more than 1,300 feet over the next 1.4 miles to the upper mine perched on an open ledge and strewn with old timbers and debris. The adit has an iron door leading to an ore cart on tracks. The adit is unstable and dangerous, so keep a safe distance.

Retrace your route to complete this scenic 6-mile round-trip in the eastern slopes and canyons of Telescope Peak.

Miles and Directions

0.0 Start at the upper trailhead/parking area 8.3 miles up Hanaupah Canyon Road.

0.6 At the springs and a mining road junction, climb to the left.

1.4 View the waterfall vista in the side canyon.

3.0 Arrive at the upper mine/adit.

6.0 Return to the trailhead for a round-trip hike. This doesn't include the distance required if you're using a two-wheel-drive vehicle.

Options: To turn this out-and-back hike into a diverse but strenuous loop, drop into the unnamed tributary canyon immediately south and east of the upper mine. Plan on three to five hours to descend this rugged and challenging canyon. It is so rugged that if you were going up, you'd quickly turn around. But with a down-canyon route, you have little choice but to keep going. You begin with a steep 500-foot drop to the canyon floor. Every twist and turn brings new surprises: sheer cliffs, formations, dry falls, and boulders that can be bypassed by climbing up, around, and back down. The midsection contains springs with pools of water in scoured rocks harboring frogs, long-eared owls, and other unlikely desert denizens. A 50-foot dry fall in the lower end forces a climb high on the left shoulder. Then more dry falls forcing more steep sidehilling. The canyon mouth intersects the trail below the upper mine and about 0.6 mile above the upper trailhead.

With its abundant water, the South Fork of Hanaupah Canyon could be used as a base camp for an extremely arduous cross-country climb of Telescope Peak (11,049 feet). The route for the gain of nearly 7,500 feet would be up the middle ridge between the South and Middle Forks of Hanaupah Canyon, intersecting the trail about 1 mile north of the peak.

20 Hummingbird Spring

An exploratory hike into a piñon-juniper canyon below Panamint Mountain cliffs takes you into a remote canyon within bighorn-sheep habitat, ending at a small spring.

See map on page 72.
Start: About 35 miles south of Stovepipe Wells Village.
Distance: 3 miles out and back.
Approximate hiking time: 1 to 2 hours.
Difficulty: Moderate.
Trail surface: Rocky path and rocky wash.

Seasons: October to mid-November, March through June.
USGS topo maps: Jail Canyon-CA and Telescope Peak-CA (1:24,000).
Trail contact: Furnace Creek Visitor Center & Museum (see appendix D).

Finding the trailhead: From California Highway 190, take Emigrant Canyon Road 20.9 miles southward to the junction with Wildrose Canyon Road. Continue east on Mahogany Flat Road, passing the ranger station and campground on the way up Wildrose Canyon. Four miles east of the campground, turn right (south) on Piñon Flat Road; there are JEEP (i.e., four-wheel drive recommended) and NO FIRES signs on a post. The gravel road becomes too rough for all but high-clearance four-wheel-drive vehicles at 1.5 miles. Park along the road and hike up the road 0.2 mile to where it bends sharply northeast and rises to the Piñon Mesa picnic area. To prevent vehicular use, stones block the old road that continues straight south. This is the trailhead.

The Hike

This hike provides exploratory opportunities for history buffs or anyone who might enjoy a destinationless ramble in a lovely remote canyon high above Death Valley. Although the spring is usually a mere trickle, the area contains dense piñon-juniper vegetation thanks to its mountainside setting. The elevation makes the hike suitable for a summertime outing in the Wildrose region of the park. Also, when the wind is intense on the ridges of the Panamints, the Hummingbird Spring valley offers some protection.

From the trailhead, the former road quickly deteriorates to a rocky trail. The area is a favorite of the resident feral burro population. Their tracks and droppings are everywhere. Avoid confrontations with these wild animals. It is unlikely that your paths would cross, since they are not interested in human contact. Whatever trail maintenance has been done in the last sixty years has been done by the burro pack that uses these pathways. The burros compete with bighorn sheep. As such, the park service will try to remove many of the burros from wild-sheep range.

As you climb the road/wash/burro path, you will spot remnants of prior human habitation: rusty cans, barrel hoops, lumber. Several pieces of galvanized pipe can be seen in the underbrush. Watch, too, for ax cuts on the pine stumps. This is a visual treasure hunt for the history detective. The actual site of the spring and buildings have vanished, but enough clues remain to suggest their whereabouts. Following the wash will bring you to a high junction of washes directly below a prominent 8,100-foot cliff face of the Panamints.

The immense value of water in the mining era in Death Valley is evident from the Skidoo Pipeline, which crosses the Mahogany Flat Road just before the Piñon Flat turnoff. This 1907 pipeline carried water from Birch Spring in Jail Canyon to the south of Telescope Peak to the town of Skidoo, 23 miles north. This project cost $250,000 (in 1907 dollars). Even a small spring like Hummingbird was important to the residents of the valley.

Exploring the various small washes and ridges that extend down from the towering cliffs of the Panamint Range behind Hummingbird Spring expands the hike and turns it into a rambling adventure. When you turn for the descent to your car, you will also enjoy vistas of Wildrose Peak and Canyon.

Miles and Directions

0.0   Head south up the eroded trail.
0.7   The trail and wash divide. Follow the one to the right.
1.5   The trail ends at a junction of three small gullies.
3.0   Return the way you came.

21 Wildrose Peak

The Wildrose Trail takes you to a high Panamint summit from which the highest and lowest land in the lower forty-eight states can be seen.

See map on page 72.
Start: About 38 miles south of Stovepipe Wells Village.
Length: 8.4 miles out and back.
Approximate hiking time: 4 to 6 hours.
Difficulty: Strenuous.
Trail surface: Dirt path.

Seasons: September to mid-November, March through June (depending on snow level).
USGS topo maps: Wildrose Peak-CA and Telescope Peak-CA (1:24,000).
Trail contact: Furnace Creek Visitor Center & Museum (see appendix D).

Finding the trailhead: From California Highway 190 at Emigrant Junction, drive south on Emigrant Canyon Road 20.9 miles to Wildrose Junction; continue east on Mahogany Flat Road (paved for 4.5 miles) and drive 7.1 miles to the Wildrose Charcoal Kilns parking area. In winter this road may be impassable; check with park authorities for weather and road conditions. The signed trail to Wildrose Peak begins at the west end of the kilns.

The Hike

Wildrose Peak provides panoramic views of Death Valley and the surrounding mountain ranges. This official park trail to Wildrose travels through classic piñon-juniper forest to a high saddle, then zigzags to the broad, open summit of this central peak in the Panamint Range. The meadowlike mountaintop is nearly always windy; appropriate clothing is a requirement, as are binoculars to enjoy the sweeping 360-degree view. Summer hikers will appreciate bug dope to combat flies and gnats.

In spite of its rather impressive elevation gain, the Wildrose Trail begins modestly. From the kilns at the trailhead, the trail charges 50 yards uphill to the northwest, achieving a 60-foot gain, but then follows the contour of the hillside for nearly the next mile. This section is a gentle warm-up for the hike ahead. Along the route, rock outcroppings extend to the west, hovering over Wildrose Canyon below. This is classic mountain-lion country.

Climbing only slightly, the trail joins another trail coming up from the canyon. Numerous pine stumps are a reminder of the logging done over a century ago to supply the charcoal kilns during their brief use in the 1870s. At the head of the canyon, the trail begins its climb. At 1.2 miles the trail bends north and steepens sharply, gaining over 600 feet in less than a mile. Rising to the first saddle, you will enjoy a magnificent view of Death Valley below through the evergreens.

The trail climbs around three small rises before emerging on a ridge above the saddle below the peak. Here, at 3.1 miles and 8,230 feet, you can pause and view the length of Death Valley. From here, a mile of switchbacks leads to the summit.

The trail snakes north, then south, then north, and so on, up the 800-foot climb. The changing direction enables you to enjoy a variety of vistas as you ascend the mountain, particularly as you near the windswept summit, which is clear of major vegetation.

A small rock wall on the peak was designed to give some protection from the wind. Or you can drop just a couple of feet down on the leeward side of the mountain to enjoy your stay and write a note for the peak registry. From Wildrose you can see the vast area of mining activity in the north end of the Panamint Range. Just to the northeast in the canyon below there is a massive mining camp. Farther along Emigrant Canyon Road, the mountainsides are crisscrossed with mining roads. Rogers (with the microwave station) and Telescope Peaks loom above to the south. To the west is the mighty wall of the Sierras. To the east, across the valley, are the Funeral and Black Mountains. This is an eagle's view of the Death Valley world.

The hike back down the mountain allows you to relax and focus on a new view of the scenery. Death Valley Canyon, extending eastward below the high saddle, is just one of the dramatic sights you may notice on the downward trip. Although this is a heavily used trail, its bending pathway preserves the sense of solitude for the hiker.

Miles and Directions

0.0 The trail climbs, then levels as it follows the contour of a hill.

0.9 Arrive at the head of Wildrose Canyon.

1.8 Arrive at a saddle, with views of Death Valley and Badwater to the east. The trail turns north and climbs to a second saddle.

2.9 Arrive at the second saddle, which offers more panoramas. The trail drops slightly, then switchbacks up the eastern side of Wildrose.

4.1 Reach the south peak, the false summit.

4.2 Reach the north peak, the genuine summit, where the register is in an ammo box.

8.4 Return to the trailhead by the same route.

22 Nemo Canyon

The Nemo Canyon hike takes you on a gentle downhill traverse hike through open desert and down a wide graveled wash, bounded by low ridges and multicolored badlands, providing a pleasing contrast to nearby mountain climbs.

Start: About 28 miles south of Stovepipe Wells Village.
Distance: 3.6 miles one way.
Approximate hiking time: 3 to 4 hours.
Difficulty: Moderate.
Trail surface: Cross-country; open graveled wash.

Seasons: October through May.
USGS topo map: Emigrant Pass-CA (1:24,000).
Trail contact: Furnace Creek Visitor Center & Museum (see appendix D).

Finding the trailhead: From Wildrose Junction (0.2 mile west of Wildrose Campground and Ranger Station), drive 2.2 miles north on the paved Emigrant Canyon Road and turn left (northwest) onto an unsigned gravel road that takes off from the paved road as it veers right (northeast). Drive 0.7 mile to the end of the road at a paved T next to a gravel pit. A USGS benchmark is adjacent to this spot, which is the trailhead/jumping-off point for the hike. The end point is the broad mouth of Nemo Canyon on Wildrose Canyon Road, down the canyon 3 miles southwest of Wildrose Junction and 1 mile southwest of the picnic area.

The Hike

This moderate point-to-point down-canyon traverse begins in open desert country dotted with creosote brush and Mormon tea. Nemo Canyon drops moderately to the southwest. To avoid walking toward the sun and into a stiff afternoon wind, make this a morning excursion if at all possible.

The canyon is wide open with low-lying hills and ridges. Soon, a few scattered yuccas begin to appear. At first the wash is braided and graveled, but it becomes better defined with a sandy bottom after about 1 mile. At 1.5 miles the valley narrows a bit. In another 0.2 mile red rhyolite bluffs rise on the left side. Around the corner the valley opens in a semicircle with several side canyons entering from the right. The white saline seep of Mud Spring is also to the right at 4,020 feet. At 2 miles 100-foot-high cliffs rise on the left as the canyon narrows slightly. After another 0.2 mile the wash parallels brightly colored badlands—red, white, black, gray, pink, and tan—with steep bluffs rising several hundred feet on the left. At 2.4 miles a huge valley enters from the right. At 3 miles and 3,550 feet, the canyon is marked by brown, deeply eroded conglomerate cliffs and spires. Soon large granite boulders appear, resting precariously atop spires of brown conglomerate. At times loose gravel impedes walking, but the steady downhill grade helps. At 3.5 miles the canyon opens to the wide Wildrose Valley. In just another 0.1 mile, Nemo Canyon meets the rough

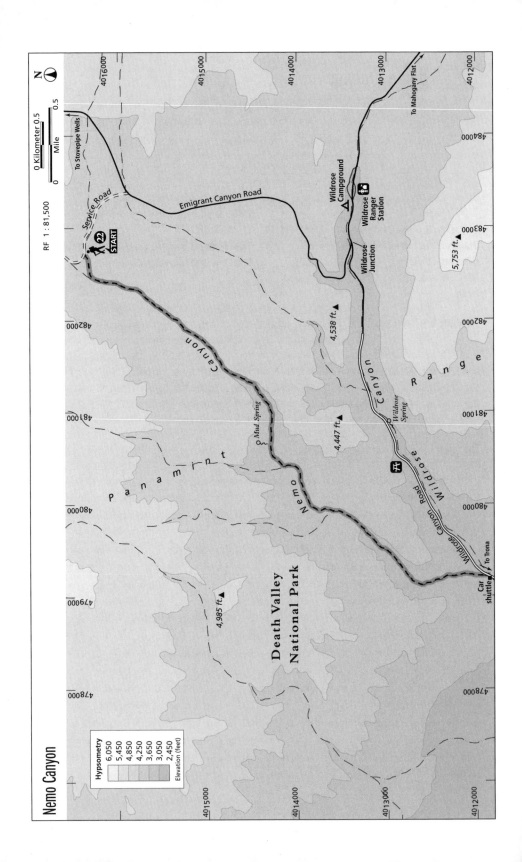

Nemo Canyon

RF 1 : 81,500

0 Kilometer 0.5

0 Mile 0.5

N

Hypsometry
6,050
5,450
4,850
4,250
3,650
3,050
2,450
Elevation (feet)

To Stovepipe Wells

Service Road

22 START

Emigrant Canyon Road

Canyon

Mud Spring

4,538 ft.▲

4,447 ft.▲

4,985 ft.▲

Panamint

Nemo

Canyon

Death Valley National Park

Wildrose Campground

Wildrose Ranger Station

Wildrose Junction

Range

Wildrose Spring

Canyon

Wildrose

Wildrose Canyon Road

To Trona

Car shuttle

To Mahogany Flat

5,753 ft.▲

Wildrose Canyon Road at 3,200 feet, thereby completing this point-to-point downhill traverse.

Miles and Directions

0.0 Start at the trailhead in the Nemo Canyon wash.

1.8 Arrive at Mud Spring.

3.6 Finish the hike at Wildrose Canyon Road.

23 Darwin Falls

A delightful moist microclimate with multitiered waterfalls is tucked away in a scenic canyon.

Start: About 31 miles southwest of Stovepipe Wells Village.

Distance: 3 miles out and back.

Approximate hiking time: 2 to 4 hours.

Difficulty: Easy to lower falls; strenuous to middle valley or overlook.

Trail surface: Dirt path to lower falls; some boulders to middle valley; primitive burro trail to overlook.

Seasons: October through June.

USGS topo map: Darwin-CA (1:24,000).

Trail contact: Furnace Creek Visitor Center & Museum (see appendix D).

Finding the trailhead: From Panamint Springs, 29.6 miles southwest of Stovepipe Wells on California Highway 190, drive west 1.1 miles to the first dirt road on the left. Turn left (south) on the dirt road and drive 2.6 miles to the signed side road on the right for the Darwin Falls parking area. You will notice a pipeline running along the road. The road is rough but passable for a standard passenger vehicle.

The Hike

Nestled at the western edge of Death Valley National Park, Darwin Falls was formerly a BLM Area of Critical Environmental Concern (ACEC). During its years of jurisdiction, the BLM took firm measures to protect the area against vehicular intrusion. Welded pipe barricades are still in place, along with stern warnings against such misuse. The BLM's 8,600-acre Darwin Falls Wilderness Area is immediately west of the park adjacent to the canyon.

Darwin Stream is the only permanent water in this area of the park. Flowing from the China Garden Spring, Darwin supplies the Panamint Springs Resort with water via a pipeline, which is visible on both the drive and the hike to the falls. This year-round water source sustains dense willow and cottonwood thickets in the valley and canyon as well as a thriving population of birds. Cliff swallows and red-tailed hawks soar overhead. Brazen chuckwalla lizards stare at intruders from their rocky lairs.

This hike is a radical change from the usual Death Valley outing. Right from the parking area, a streak of greenery and a glistening brook lead up the gently sloping valley floor. Hopping from one side of the stream to the other begins here and will continue throughout the hike. Steady footwork will prevent getting soaked, but care is especially required on the smooth, slippery boulders farther up the canyon. The Darwin Mountains of black rhyolite tower above the bright green grass, the willow saplings, the horsetails and cattails.

At the notch of the canyon's mouth, another welded barricade remains, as does a BLM sign reminding visitors of Darwin Falls' value to vegetation and to wildlife. Bathing and wading are prohibited. The high, dry trail is above the stream on the south side of the canyon. There are many bends in the narrow canyon. With the steep canyon walls, as well as the willow and cottonwood thickets, this is a shady hike, an excellent outing for a hot sunny day! A USGS gauging station is on the north side of the stream. With its aluminum phone booth architecture, it looks decidedly out of place in this Garden of Eden. Beyond the station you need to watch your footing when clambering over the smooth water-eroded boulders.

At 1 mile, after hearing them in the distance, you reach the falls. Double falls cascade over a 25-foot dropoff, surrounded by large old cottonwoods. Sword ferns, watercress, and cattails flourish in the pool below the falls. This is the turnaround point for the shorter hike.

To continue the recommended hike, retreat 50 yards downstream and pick up the use trail up the south wall. The best option (there are several use trails) takes off on a solid outcropping of greenish granite and traverses the canyon wall to the valley above the falls. Climbing the finely grained granite must be done with caution. It doesn't crumble, but it can be very slippery. From the trail, thread your way through the dense willows and cottonwoods to the upper end of the valley adjacent to a very loose talus slope. Here the three-tiered upper falls plummet 140 feet from the cliff above. This is not a heavily visited spot. In the narrow canyon your only company will probably be the cliff swallows swooping overhead.

To continue to the overlook, return down the valley to the same route and follow the burros' use trail on up the canyon's south wall. The trail emerges 140 feet above the valley. From the pinnacle at the point where the stream bends sharply from its easterly flow to a northern direction is the only view of the highest fall. Here the stream takes an 80-foot clear drop. This is the turnaround point for the longer hike.

Emerging from Darwin Canyon is an Alice-in-Wonderland experience. After being surrounded by humidity and greenery, the beige world of the desert looks one-dimensional. The valley below the canyon is a striking transition zone, with the soft greenery of the stream ecosystem juxtaposed against the jagged dark rhyolite cliffs of the mountains to the south. The hike to Darwin Falls is a carnival of sensory perceptions. The smells, sounds, feel, and sight of this watery world make this an exceptional experience.

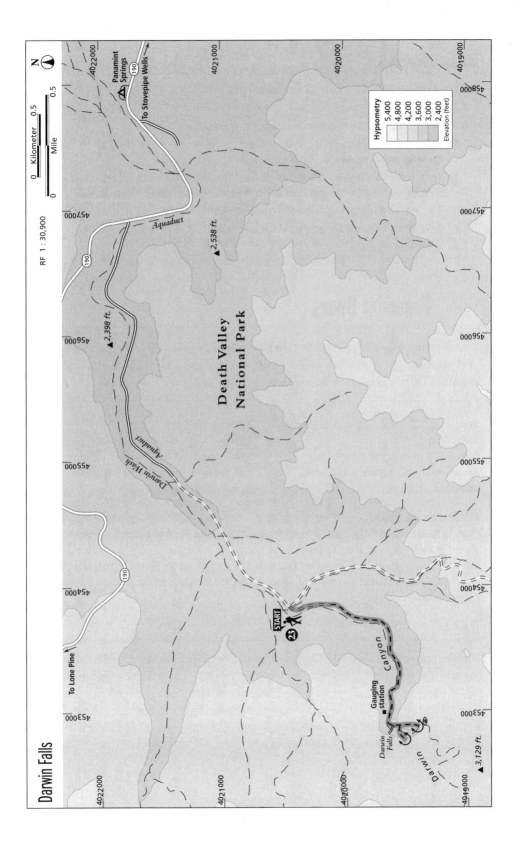

Darwin Falls

RF 1 : 30,900

N

0   Kilometer   0.5

0   Mile   0.5

To Lone Pine

To Stovepipe Wells

Panamint Springs

190

Aquaduct

2,398 ft.

2,538 ft.

Darwin Wash

Aquaduct

Death Valley National Park

START

23

Gauging station

Canyon

Darwin Falls

Darwin

3,129 ft.

Hypsometry

5,400
4,800
4,200
3,600
3,000
2,400

Elevation (feet)

Miles and Directions

0.0–0.4 The trail follows a stream up the narrow valley floor.

0.4 There's a vehicle barricade at the entrance to the canyon.

0.9 A USGS stream-gauging station is located on the right bank.

1.0 Arrive at the lower falls. Drop back downstream 50 yards to pick up the trail to the middle valley and overlook.

1.1 Arrive at the middle valley and thread your way through the willows to the high basin and pools below the falls (at 1 mile). Return to the same trail to ascend to the overlook.

1.4 Take the burro use trail to a view of the highest falls.

1.6 Arrive at the falls overlook and the turnaround point.

3.0 Return to the trailhead.

24 Panamint Dunes

This is a cross-country open desert hike on relatively inaccessible, high, star-shaped sand dunes in the expanded western region of the park. Spectacular views of the Panamint Valley and surrounding mountain ranges sweep in all directions.

Start: About 30 miles southwest of Stovepipe Wells Village.
Distance: 9 miles out and back.
Approximate hiking time: 3 to 4 hours.
Difficulty: Moderate.

Trail surface: Sand. No trail.
Seasons: Mid-October to mid-April.
USGS topo map: The Dunes-CA (1:24,000).
Trail contact: Furnace Creek Visitor Center & Museum (see appendix D).

Finding the trailhead: From Panamint Springs, drive east on California Highway 190 for 4.9 miles to the signed Lake Hill Road. Turn left (north) on Lake Hill Road and drive 6.1 miles to where the road begins to deteriorate as it bends east. This is the north end of the North Panamint Dry Lake bed. Park on the left (west) side of the road at the bend and begin the hike from here. The access road is rough and graveled but can be negotiated by standard vehicles driven slowly and carefully.

The Hike

The Panamint Dunes are clearly visible to the northwest from the trailhead/parking area. Because these extensive dunes rise several hundred feet, they appear deceptively close. In fact, they are 4 miles away across open desert, requiring a steady one-and-a-half- to two-hour walk just to reach the higher complex of dunes. This relative inaccessibility, as compared to most other dunes in the California desert region, accounts for their pristine quality.

Hiking the Panamint Dunes with a view to the northeast—star-shaped dune configurations are visible on the north side of these dunes.

These ever-changing mounds of sand are home to several endemic plants, dune grass, vetch, and more. The Panamint Valley is the site of mysterious rock alignments, some of which are called "intaglios." Intaglios are of prehistoric human origin and are huge animal shapes, perhaps hundreds of feet in size. These shapes, one of which is reported to be of a hummingbird, can be discerned from an airplane but not from the dunes. Fortunately, the park wilderness designation now protects these artifacts from the destructive impact of off-road vehicles.

At first the line-of-sight cross-country route to the dunes crosses a short section of rough, rocky alluvial fan. Don't be discouraged, for soon the open desert floor is made up mostly of well-compacted sand and desert pavement with more solid footing. The ascent is gradual, averaging only about 250 feet per mile. At 2.5 miles and 2,020 feet elevation, you'll reach the lower edge of the dunes, with large creosote bushes dominating the landscape. The going becomes a bit slower in the softer sand.

After another mile and 400-foot ascent, the base of the higher dunes is attained. Dune grass appears in sporadic patches with the indentations of animal and insect tracks seemingly everywhere. From here pick out a sandy ridge route to the apex of

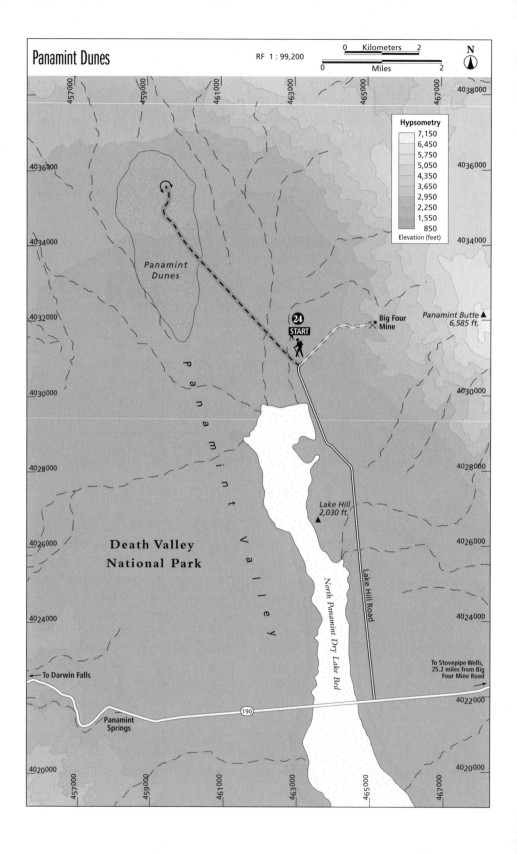

Panamint Dunes

RF 1 : 99,200

Kilometers
0   2

Miles
0   2

N

Hypsometry

Elevation (feet)
7,150
6,450
5,750
5,050
4,350
3,650
2,950
2,250
1,550
850

Panamint Dunes

24
START

Big Four
Mine

Panamint Butte ▲
6,585 ft.

P a n a m i n t   V a l l e y

Lake Hill
2,030 ft.
▲

**Death Valley
National Park**

North Panamint Dry Lake Bed

Lake Hill Road

← To Darwin Falls

To Stovepipe Wells,
25.2 miles from Big
Four Mine Road

190

Panamint
Springs

the dunes, attained after another mile, somewhere around 2,700 feet elevation. Depending on angle to the wind and relative moisture, climbing the nearly 300-foot-high dunes can be tiring, but the effort by way of a route of swirling, twisting ridges to the top will be well rewarded.

The star-shaped configuration of these dunes is especially apparent on the northern backside. Here swirls of sand wrap around small circular basins and bowls forming an intricate maze of shapes and patterns. Some of the sand basins resemble perfectly rounded craters. The view from the knife-ridge apex of the dunes is magnificent. Panamint Springs can be seen far to the southwest. The vast Panamint Valley stretches southward with the distinctive volcanic remnants of Lake Hill rising from the dry lake bed. Lofty Telescope Peak crowns the Panamint Mountains, with the multicolored bands of Panamint Butte dominating the immediate southeast horizon.

To return, follow a line-of-sight route toward Telescope Peak—by far the highest point to the south—and you'll end up at or very close to the trailhead, thereby completing this varied 9-mile trip to the Panamint Dunes. At first glance you might think that all dunes are somewhat similar, just another "pile of sand" as we heard one casual observer to say. Not so. Each of the four dune hikes suggested in this book, and their desert basin and range settings, is so different from the others that they can hardly be compared.

Miles and Directions

0.0 At the north end of the North Panamint Dry Lake bed, begin the hike across open, sandy desert.

2.5 After a gradual ascent you'll reach the lower edge of the dunes, with creosote bushes dominating.

3.5 Reach the base of the higher dunes (2,420 feet).

4.5 Reach the high point of the dunes (2,700 feet).

9.0 Return to the trailhead.

25 Marble Canyon

Marble Canyon is a long out-and-back day hike up a deep, narrow canyon in the Cottonwood Mountains. Here you will find colorful rock formations, petroglyphs, and expansive views of remote backcountry.

Start: About 14 miles west of Stovepipe Wells Village.
Distance: 9.6 miles out and back from the road closure 2.6 miles up Marble Canyon Road (if your vehicle is parked at the signed Cottonwood-Marble Canyon junction, add 5.2 miles to the round-trip hiking distance).
Approximate hiking time: 4 to 5 hours, or 7 to 8 hours for longer outing.

Difficulty: Moderate.
Trail surface: Rocky path for 1.1 miles; sandy wash thereafter.
Seasons: October through May.
USGS topo map: Cottonwood Creek-CA (1:24,000).
Trail contact: Furnace Creek Visitor Center & Museum (see appendix D).

Finding the trailhead: From Stovepipe Wells Village on California Highway 190, head west on Cottonwood Road. Cottonwood Road begins by bearing left at the entrance to the Stovepipe Wells Campground. The two-wheel-drive portion of this slow, rocky road ends after 8.4 miles when the road drops steeply into Cottonwood Wash and turns left up the canyon. High-clearance four-wheel drive is advised beyond this point due to soft gravel and high centers. The junction of Cottonwood and Marble Canyon Roads is 10.7 miles from the Stovepipe Wells Campground. Cottonwood Canyon is to the left. Marble Canyon Road continues to the right another 2.6 miles to the signed vehicle closure at the canyon narrows, but park at the junction if you have any doubts about whether your vehicle can negotiate these final very rough 2.6 miles.

The Hike

The adjacent Cottonwood and Marble Canyons are as different from each other as night and day. Cottonwood is wide and open whereas Marble is a wonderland of intimate narrows and dark alcoves.

The recommended trip described below is an out-and-back exploration of scenic Marble Canyon all the way up to its junction with Dead Horse Canyon. However, a much longer 23-mile backpacking loop through both canyons can be undertaken by those willing to cache water on this dry route and commit a minimum of three days. The loop can start from the Cottonwood/Marble Canyon Road junction. Begin by hiking 8.5 miles up the Cottonwood Canyon road, cross over into Marble Canyon by way of Dead Horse Canyon, and descend 7.4 miles down Marble Canyon from the mouth of Dead Horse Canyon to the point of origin at the road junction. About half of this loop is on open four-wheel-drive roads, with

Marble Canyon contains several sets of petroglyphs—
look but don't touch. ▶

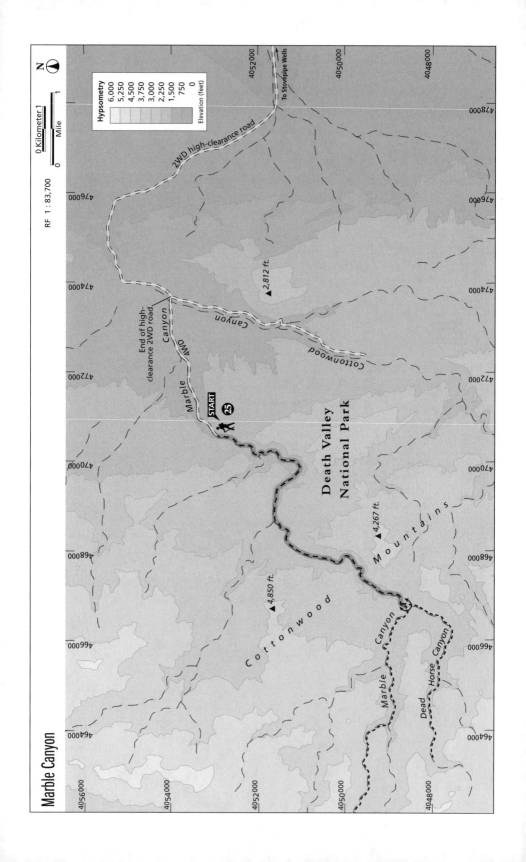

Marble Canyon

RF 1 : 83,700

N

0 Kilometer 1
0 Mile 1

Hypsometry
6,000
5,250
4,500
3,750
3,000
2,250
1,500
750
0
Elevation (feet)

To Stovepipe Wells

2WD high-clearance road

End of high-clearance 2WD road

Marble   Canyon

4WD

Cottonwood   Canyon

▲ 2,812 ft.

START
25

Death Valley
National Park

▲ 4,850 ft.

Cottonwood

Marble

Dead Horse Canyon

Canyon

▲ 4,267 ft.

Mountains

the remainder being canyon washes and an overland cross-country route. Marble Canyon is susceptible to flash flooding with a corresponding danger of being caught in one of its steep chutes with no escape. Do not attempt to hike the canyon if wet weather appears imminent.

For the Marble Canyon out-and-back day excursion, the hike might start out of vehicular necessity at the Cottonwood/Marble Canyons Road junction, but the real adventure begins 2.6 miles up at the canyon gap/road closure. On the way up at mile 2.3, petroglyphs can be seen at the mouth of the canyon. Sadly, some of these irreplaceable cultural links to the past have been senselessly defaced by vandals. There are more pristine petroglyphs farther up Marble Canyon, readily seen going up but more difficult to spot on the way down.

At the trailhead the canyon is only about 6 feet wide, coinciding with the wilderness boundary, which is signed with a closure to vehicular travel. At 0.3 mile a canyon enters from the right, which leads quickly to a 15-foot dry fall. Continue left up the creosote–Mormon tea bottom next to great stair-step beds of tilted gray and red rock. At 1.1 miles a huge boulder blocks the canyon—it can be bypassed on the right by climbing up stepping stones. At 1.3 miles the canyon narrows to sheer, gray cliffs where graffiti mars still more petroglyphs. Here every turn in the twisting canyon brings new variety, with arches being formed from smooth, gently eroded gray cliffs. Overhangs create an almost cavelike effect.

At 1.6 miles the valley opens dramatically only to narrow again at 1.9 miles. Once more the valley widens with brilliant displays of reds, tans, and grays on both sides at 2.3 miles. Here a major canyon enters from the right; stay to the left (west) by entering dark-walled narrows, which soon give way to a long, open stretch. The canyon closes in again at 3.5 miles, marked by a distinctive semicircular alcove on the left. Soon white and gray bands of marble resembling zebra stripes border a wonderland of grottos in the narrow canyon. A second large boulder blocks the wash at 4 miles but can be easily bypassed by climbing a "staircase" rock on the left. A small side canyon, overlooked by buttes and pinnacles, enters on the right at 4.2 miles.

Dead Horse Canyon joins Marble Canyon from the left (south) at 4.8 miles, at an elevation of 3,110 feet. The wide Dead Horse Valley looks deceptively like the main drainage, but Marble Canyon cuts sharply to the right (west). There are several spacious and excellent campsites at this junction, above the wash, for those willing to pack sufficient water for an overnight stay.

Many years ago someone etched GOLD BELT SPRING 4 MILES into the desert varnish of a large rock with an arrow pointing up Marble Canyon. Another 0.2 mile above the junction a massive white cliff oversees the left side of Marble Canyon as it climbs steeply toward Goldbelt Spring.

As you return down the canyon to the trailhead, you'll appreciate having had the sun at your back both for the morning ascent and the afternoon descent. This trip is well worth a full day of canyon exploration.

Miles and Directions

0.0 The trailhead is at a signed vehicle closure 2.6 miles up the Marble Canyon Road, where canyon walls are only 6 or 7 feet apart.

0.3 Where the canyon (right) leads to a 15-foot dry fall, stay left.

1.1 A huge boulder blocks the canyon, ending the previously open four-wheel-drive road. Climb up the stepping stones to the right.

1.4 Overhangs here create a cavelike effect in the canyon.

2.3 At the major junction, continue left (west) into a narrow, dark-walled canyon.

3.5 The canyon again narrows, with a semicircular alcove on the right.

4.0 Another boulder blocks the canyon. Climb the staircase of rocks on the left.

4.8 Dead Horse Canyon enters from the south; turnaround point.

9.6 Return to the trailhead.

26 Mosaic Canyon

Patterned walls of multicolored rock and water–sculpted formations await you in this picturesque canyon near Stovepipe Wells.

Start: About 2 miles south of Stovepipe Wells Village.
Distance: 3.6 miles out and back.
Approximate hiking time: 2 to 3 hours.
Difficulty: Easy to lower dry fall; moderate to upper dry fall.

Trail surface: Dirt path with rock, then open canyon floor.
Seasons: October through April.
USGS topo map: Stovepipe Wells-CA (1:24,000).
Trail contact: Furnace Creek Visitor Center & Museum (see appendix D).

Finding the trailhead: From California Highway 190, 0.1 mile southwest of Stovepipe Wells Village, head south on the rough but passable Mosaic Canyon Road (signed). After 2.1 miles the road ends at the Mosaic Canyon parking area and the trail takes off immediately (south).

The Hike

The fault in the Tucki Mountain that produced Mosaic Canyon consists of mosaic breccia and smooth Noonday formation dolomite, formed in a sea bed 750 million to 900 million years ago. After being pressurized and baked at more than 1,000 degrees, then eroded, the resulting rock has startling contrasts of both texture and color.

Hikers make their way through the marbleized
watercourse of Mosaic Canyon.

Mosaic Canyon; Grotto Canyon; Little Bridge Canyon

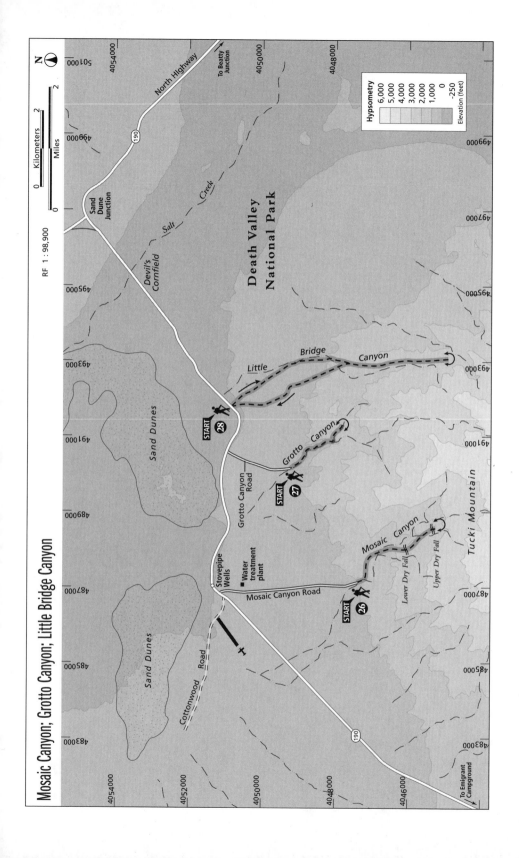

Mosaic Canyon drains more than 4 square miles of the Tucki Range, so it is to be avoided, like all canyons, in flash-flood conditions. Rushing water, carrying its load of scouring boulders, has created smooth marbleized waterways out of the otherwise lumpy breccia. Silky surfaces gradually change to ragged lumps from the canyon floor up its walls, reflecting the varying depths of floodwaters.

Like other canyons in Tucki Mountain, Mosaic Canyon is alternately wide and narrow. The wider spots are more numerous, and are broad enough almost to qualify as valleys. Often parties of hikers arrive at these open areas and turn back, figuring that the canyon excitement has ended. With plenty of water and a broad-brimmed hat, you can continue exploring the depths of Mosaic. If it's a hot day, be aware that this is not a deep, shady canyon like the ones in the Grapevine and Funeral Mountains.

The first 0.2 mile of canyon features the smooth marble surfaces that have made Mosaic a favorite destination of Death Valley visitors. After that, the canyon opens to a wide colorful amphitheater, swinging eastward to a broad valley with a 40-foot butte standing in the center. Use trails go in all directions, converging at the end of the valley where the canyon narrows again. To the right of this butte, a deep wash will eventually become a new branch of Mosaic Canyon.

At 1 mile a small pile of boulders blocks a narrow spot. A well-traveled path to the left provides an easy detour. After another wide spot, the canyon narrows again, where an abrupt 40-foot dry fall blocks your passage. It is possible to get around this barrier by way of a well-traveled and cairned trail. Drop 50 yards back from the dry fall to the trail on the sloping canyon wall to the south. This trail takes you to the upper region of Mosaic Canyon where another 0.5 mile of marbleized chutes and narrows awaits you. A steep marble chute, 50 feet high, halts the hike at 1.8 miles. It's a striking spot, with eroding, fragmented Tucki Mountain rising above the silky smooth waterslide.

The hike back down the canyon provides new views of Death Valley and the Cottonwood Mountains in the distance. Sliding down the short water chutes on the return to the trailhead increases the marbleized beauty of these breccia formations; generations of hikers have added to water's erosive force in creating these smooth rocks.

Miles and Directions

0.0–0.2 The trail begins in a wash from the parking area behind an information sign.

0.2 Hike through the wide-open canyon.

1.4 A 40-foot dry fall blocks the canyon; 50 yards back, cairns and arrows mark the side trail detour.

1.8 A 50-foot marble chute blocks the canyon.

2.8 Return to the trailhead from the lower dry fall.

3.6 Return to the trailhead from the upper dry fall.

27 Grotto Canyon

This out-and-back canyon hike winds through water-carved grottos and narrows of polished rock to a high, dry falls.

See map on page 96.
Start: About 3.5 miles southeast of Stovepipe Wells Village.
Distance: 4 miles out and back.
Approximate hiking time: 2 to 3 hours.
Difficulty: Easy.

Trail surface: Sandy rocky wash, then open canyon floor.
Seasons: October through April.
USGS topo map: Grotto Canyon-CA (1:24,000).
Trail contact: Furnace Creek Visitor Center & Museum (see appendix D).

Finding the trailhead: The Grotto Canyon access road heads south from California Highway 190, 2.4 miles east of Stovepipe Wells Village. The road is signed for Grotto Canyon and four-wheel-drive vehicles. After 1.1 miles the road ends for most vehicles above the wash, which is soft gravel. There's no actual trailhead, but the road/trail continues on up the wash to the canyon.

The Hike

With careful driving, a passenger vehicle can negotiate the road to the wash on the Grotto Canyon hike. The soft gravel of the wash for the mile to the canyon entrance requires high clearance and four-wheel drive. No signs or markers punctuate the end of the road, but severe washouts end vehicle access just before the first dry fall. Conditions in this canyon change with each flood. At times the gravel is deep and the dry falls are easy to scale, but often floods have scoured the gravel away, making exploring more of a challenge.

Like the other Tucki Mountain canyons, Grotto is a very broad canyon, up to 200 yards wide in many areas. Deeply eroded canyon walls stand like medieval castle ramparts, with short serpentine pathways in their lower reaches. The narrows at 1.8 miles bring welcome shade after the journey up the graveled canyon bottom. A pair of ravens nesting in the aerie alcove above the grotto may provide suitable visual and sound effects for the hiker approaching the almost cavelike section of the canyon. About 0.1 mile back down the canyon, a cairned trail on the eastern side leads you around this barrier to the canyon above. Another dry fall will block your travels there, so start your return trip.

Even with its proximity to Stovepipe Wells, Grotto Canyon is not heavily visited. Thus the adventuresome hiker can enjoy desert exploration and solitude without a lengthy drive. The high silence above Mesquite Flat rings in your ears—between cries of the ravens.

The narrows of Grotto Canyon.

Hiking back to the road, the dunes stretch out below, framed by the Cottonwood and Grapevine Mountains. Grotto Canyon is a desert wonder of a smaller dimension.

Miles and Directions

0.0–0.8 There's no actual trailhead, so from your car hike up the gravel jeep road in the wash.

1.8 Arrive at the narrows.

2.0 Turn back where another dry fall blocks your path.

4.0 Return to the trailhead.

28 Little Bridge Canyon

As its name suggests, this canyon has a natural bridge, as well as an arch. The hike can be done as either a loop or out and back across a broad alluvial fan.

See map on page 96.
Start: About 3 miles east of Stovepipe Wells Village.
Distance: 7 mile loop.
Approximate hiking time: 3 to 4 hours.
Difficulty: Strenuous.

Trail surface: Cross-country on rocky alluvial fan, open canyon floor.
Seasons: Mid-October through April.
USGS topo map: Grotto Canyon-CA (1:24,000).
Trail contact: Furnace Creek Visitor Center & Museum (see appendix D).

Finding the trailhead: The unsigned trailhead/route takes off to the south from California Highway 190 between Stovepipe Wells and the junction of CA 190 and Scotty's Castle Road. Little Bridge is the first major canyon east of the signed Grotto Canyon Road. The actual starting point/pullout on CA 190 is 3 miles east of Stovepipe Wells.

The Hike

Little Bridge Canyon isn't deep and narrow but it does contain several hidden points of wonder, making its exploration interesting and enjoyable. Unlike nearby Grotto and Mosaic Canyons, it is lightly visited, primarily because you must hike about 2.5 miles across a graveled alluvial fan just to reach the canyon entrance. One way to add a bit of spice to these first couple of open desert miles is to approach Little Bridge Canyon by way of a southeast-trending gully that parallels the steep mountain slopes on the right (west). By hiking up this gully, then up Little Bridge

The Little Bridge of the canyon of the same name about ▶
1 mile up from the canyon mouth.

Canyon, and returning to the trailhead/parking area back down the alluvial fan, a loop of about 7 miles can be attained without increasing the round-trip distance of a less interesting out-and-back route.

Begin the hike by heading south to southeast across desert pavement then up the alluvial fan toward the power line and the Little Bridge Canyon entrance, which cannot be seen from the highway. Soon after passing under the power line at 0.5 mile, you'll enter a deep, graveled wash. At 1 mile the route reaches a high-walled wash where the walking becomes more difficult in loose gravel. Soon a major canyon enters from the right; continue southward up the left-hand wash. At 1.5 miles the wash narrows; climb to the left over a 5-foot dry fall. A 12-foot fall appears around the bend. Backtrack a short distance and take a faint use trail on the right side (going up), which climbs and then drops above the dry fall. Soon the wash narrows to only 3 or 4 feet.

At 1.9 miles large boulders block a narrow gap; climb around to the left with rock walls rising on the right. At 2 miles the canyon opens up, with its head being reached at 2.3 miles just south of Little Bridge Canyon.

The sand dunes of Mesquite Flat can be seen back to the north, with Little Bridge straight ahead and to the right. Drop 20 feet into the wide wash, turn right, and enter the red-walled Little Bridge Canyon entrance at 2.4 miles. At 2.5 miles the canyon narrows a bit, bounded by bright red walls. Compared to most Death Valley canyons, this one runs due north straight as an arrow. Striking clefts of white quartzite appear on the right at 2.7 miles, contrasting dramatically with adjacent dark rhyolite. Loose gravel makes for tiring walking, but the effort is soon rewarded with a small arch on the right (west) side at 3 miles.

At 3.1 miles a sizable canyon suitable for a side trip enters from the right. At 3.4 miles the main canyon again narrows, with a large cave high on the right side and the namesake natural bridge of Little Bridge Canyon also on the right side. This stunning sweep of white quartzite has a 20-foot-high opening bounded by a 40-foot-high arch. The notch above and to the right of the natural bridge ends quickly at a dry fall but provides a photographic angle for the bridge. With juniper clinging to the cliffs, this is indeed a tranquil and picturesque spot.

Hike up the canyon another 0.1 mile to a white quartzite gap for expansive views of the dunes northward and of great mounds of dark rhyolite rock overhead. The canyon narrows above but can be hiked for several more miles by those with sufficient time, energy, and water. To return, hike back down the canyon past the junction point with the side gully route. Continue to the right down the canyon and gradually angle left across the alluvial fan toward the sand dunes, aiming toward the highway/parking area starting point, to complete this adventurous 7-mile round-trip loop.

Miles and Directions

0.0 From the starting point on CA 190, head southeast up an alluvial fan toward Little Bridge Canyon.

0.5 Pass under a power line.

0.6 Enter a deep graveled wash.

1.0 At the high-walled gravel wash, continue up the left-hand side.

1.5 Where the wash narrows, climb left past a 5-foot dry fall.

1.6 At the 12-foot dry fall, climb a faint use trail to the right.

2.3 Reach the head of a gully just south of the mouth of Little Bridge Canyon.

2.4 Arrive at the mouth of Little Bridge Canyon.

3.0 Reach a small arch on the right (west) side of the wide wash/canyon.

3.4 Stop and observe the natural bridge on the right side of the canyon.

3.5 The canyon narrows above and can be hiked for several more miles.

7.0 Return to the trailhead.

29 Salt Creek Interpretive Trail

A nature trail on a boardwalk along Salt Creek features pupfish, pickleweed, and salt grass, and an optional 5-mile hike north to Devil's Cornfield.

Start: About 14 miles north of Furnace Creek.
Distance: 0.5 mile lollipop.
Approximate hiking time: Less than 1 hour.
Difficulty: Easy.
Trail surface: Boardwalk; use trail to Devil's Cornfield.
Seasons: November through April.

USGS topo maps: Beatty Junction-CA (Salt Creek Nature Trail), Stovepipe Wells Northeast-CA, and Grotto Canyon-CA (5-mile one-way hike), (1:24,000).
Trail contact: Furnace Creek Visitor Center & Museum (see appendix D).

Finding the trailhead: From California Highway 190, 2.4 miles northwest of Beatty Junction and 4 miles south of Sand Dune Junction, turn southwest on Salt Creek Road and drive 1.2 miles to the Salt Creek Interpretive Trail. From the park visitor center in Furnace Creek, drive north on California Highway 190 for 13.8 miles and turn left on the signed Salt Creek Road, 1.2 miles to its end.

The end point on the one-way hike to Devil's Cornfield is where Sand Dunes Road joins CA 190 from the north, 6.3 miles east of Stovepipe Wells Village and 1.1 miles west of Sand Dune Junction, on the south side of the highway across from Sand Dunes Road.

Salt Creek's boardwalk trail runs along the stream full of pupfish.

The Hike

Salt Creek Interpretive Trail is a fully accessible lollipop-shaped boardwalk hike, with trailside signs providing interpretive information. The extended hike continues 4.5 miles up Salt Creek to the Devil's Cornfield on CA 190. There is a beachlike quality to the short hike, not only due to the boardwalk designed to protect this delicate habitat, but also due to the aroma of salt water and the salt grass and pickleweed growing in dense clumps on the sandy stream banks.

The Salt Creek pupfish, endemic to Death Valley, are the stars of this hike. In the spring there are hundreds of them in the riffles and pools of the creek. In other seasons they are dormant (winter) or the stream is reduced to isolated pools (summer and fall).

The boardwalk runs alongside the creek and then crosses it in several spots, so it provides an excellent vantage point to watch the pupfish in the clear shallow water or the deep pools. Pupfish are small (not much longer than an inch) and fast, and enjoy zipping up and down the shallow riffles to bunch up in schools in the deeper terminal pools. As prehistoric Lake Manly dried up and grew saltier, these little fish

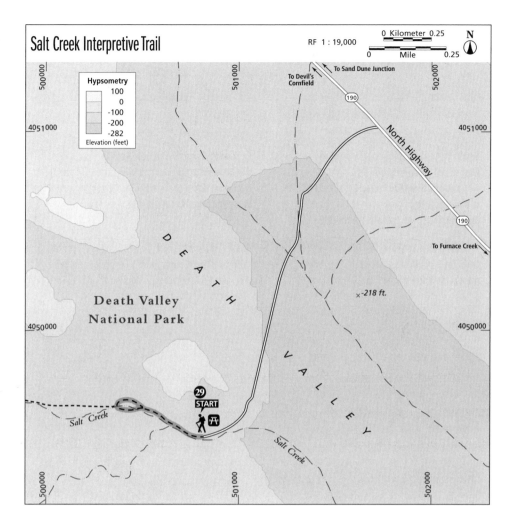

RF 1 : 19,000

0 Kilometer 0.25

0 Mile 0.25

N

Hypsometry
100
0
-100
-200
-282
Elevation (feet)

To Sand Dune Junction

To Devil's
Cornfield

190

North Highway

4051000

4051000

To Furnace Creek

D E A T H

**Death Valley
National Park**

x *-218 ft.*

4050000

4050000

V A L L E Y

**29
START**

Salt Creek

Salt Creek

500000

501000

502000

500000

501000

502000

were able to adapt to the new salty environment. Slimy green and brown algae, caddis flies, beetles, and water boatmen flourish here, too, providing an adequate diet for the pupfish.

The walk out along Salt Creek is a startling change from the usual Death Valley desert-floor hike. The sound of the merry running water in the winter and spring, with the flourishing growth of salt grasses, suggests a stroll on the beach. All that's missing are the seagulls. With the interpretive signs along the trail, you can enjoy the fish and birds as well as learn about the dynamic changes of the desert habitat and the ability of some species to adapt to its harsh conditions.

Option: To undertake the one-way hike up Salt Creek (which disappears at 2 miles), take the use trail from the far end of the loop, heading north to CA 190 at the Sand Dunes Road. Make sure your car shuttle is reliable because you won't feel like reversing your route to Salt Creek.

30 Titus Canyon Narrows

This narrow canyon cut deeply into the Grapevine Mountains is dominated by majestic cliffs and arched caverns.

Start: About 32 miles north of Furnace Creek.
Distance: 4.2 miles out and back.
Approximate hiking time: 2 to 3 hours.
Difficulty: Easy.
Trail surface: Rocky four-wheel-drive road.

Seasons: October through April.
USGS topo map: Fall Canyon-CA (1:24,000).
Trail contact: Furnace Creek Visitor Center & Museum (see appendix D).

Finding the trailhead: The two-way road to the mouth of Titus Canyon is 11.9 miles north of Daylight Pass Road (Nevada Highway 374) and California 190 junction, and 17.9 miles south of the Grapevine Ranger Station on Scotty's Castle Road. Take the signed dirt road northeast 2.7 miles up the alluvial fan to the Titus Canyon mouth, where there is a parking area.

The Hike

Titus Canyon is the longest and one of the grandest canyons in Death Valley. Titus Canyon Road was built in 1926 to serve the town of Leadville, an investor scam that became a ghost town the following year. This 26-mile one-way unpaved road was washed away by winter floods in 2004. The only way to visit majestic Titus Canyon is now by foot. The rough 2-mile portion at the western end of Titus Road still exists. From there you can park and hike the dramatic narrows of the canyon. Driving to the canyon mouth also enables you to omit the alluvial-fan hike that's so common in canyon hiking in Death Valley.

Titus Canyon is a slot canyon, immediately narrow at its mouth. From the brightness of the desert floor, you are plunged into the cool shadows of the canyon. Cliffs tower hundreds of feet above. Breezes rush down through the funnel of the canyon. The display of cliffs continues without intermission for 2 miles as you hike up the primitive canyon road. The variety of colors and textures on the canyon walls is immense and ever-changing. The limestone layers are twisted and folded; fault lines run at all angles. In addition to the power of the earth's surface to rise and fall and shift, the power of water is visible throughout the slot canyon. The water-smoothed walls indicate the level of flooding. The curves of the canyon's path reveal the erosive power of the swift floods as they roar down the narrow opening with their load of scouring boulders. Flash floods are a real danger in Titus, as 2004 demonstrated.

The 2-mile hike through the narrows is overpowering. Like walking down the nave of a European cathedral, hiking up (and later down) Titus is a soaring experience, but also an immensely humbling one. The Titus Canyon Fault, which created the

The canyon walls in lower Titus Canyon dwarf hikers.

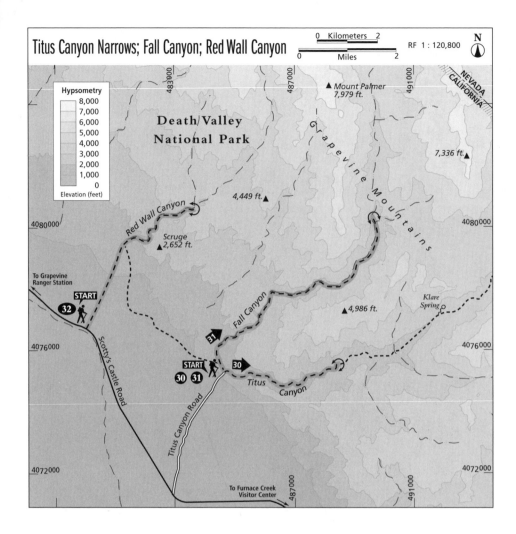

0   Kilometers   2

0   Miles   2

RF 1 : 120,800

N

Hypsometry

8,000
7,000
6,000
5,000
4,000
3,000
2,000
1,000
0
Elevation (feet)

Death Valley
National Park

▲ Mount Palmer
7,979 ft.

7,336 ft. ▲

Grapevine Mountains

Red Wall Canyon

4,449 ft. ▲

4080000

Scruge
▲ 2,652 ft.

4080000

To Grapevine
Ranger Station

START

32

Fall Canyon

Klare
Spring ○

31

▲ 4,986 ft.

4076000

Scotty's Castle Road

START

30 **31**

30

Titus Canyon

4076000

4072000

Titus Canyon Road

To Furnace Creek
Visitor Center

4072000

canyon, slices through the heart of the Grapevine Mountains, laying their innards
bare for the geologist and layman both to enjoy.

Miles and Directions

0.0   From the canyon mouth, follow the four-wheel-drive road east into Titus Canyon.

2.1   The narrow canyon opens into a broader valley. Turn around here.

4.2   Retrace your steps to the parking area.

Option: For a longer and more strenuous hike—a total of 12 miles and five to six
hours—continue up the road another 4 miles to Klare Spring. The canyon floor is
considerably broader, although quite steep, after passing from the narrows at 2.1
miles, but the towering peaks of the Grapevines provide a spectacular backdrop for
this canyon hike. The spring is on the north side of the road. It's a critical habitat for

bighorn sheep, which gather nearby in hot summer months. Some marred petroglyphs are above the spring, a reminder that it is both unlawful and boorish to harm such artifacts. Return the way you came, enjoying your downhill trip.

31 Fall Canyon

This twisting, deep canyon in the colorful Grapevine Mountains features one of the most spectacular canyon narrows in the park.

See map on page 108.
Start: About 32 miles north of Furnace Creek.
Distance: 16 miles out and back.
Approximate hiking time: 4 to 5 hours.
Difficulty: Strenuous.

Trail surface: Sandy path and cross-country on a clear wash.
Seasons: October through April.
USGS topo map: Fall Canyon-CA (1:24,000).
Trail contact: Furnace Creek Visitor Center & Museum (see appendix D).

Finding the trailhead: The trailhead is at the Titus Canyon mouth parking area 2.7 miles north of Scotty's Castle Road on Titus Canyon Road. The two-way road to the mouth of Titus Canyon takes off 11.9 miles north of the California Highway 374/190 junction and 17.9 miles south of the Grapevine Ranger Station on Scotty's Castle Road. Proceed northeast on the signed Titus Canyon dirt road 2.7 miles up the alluvial fan to the mouth of Titus Canyon, where there is a parking area. Right behind the trailhead restroom, follow the distinct but unsigned trail north of the parking area 0.7 mile to an extensive wash leading to the mouth of Fall Canyon.

The Hike

Do not attempt this hike if wet weather appears likely. Fall Canyon is highly susceptible to flash flooding. You could easily be trapped in one of the narrow stretches of the canyon by a raging torrent if caught during a mountain storm.

From the parking area at the mouth of Titus Canyon, hike north on an unsigned but easy to follow use trail, climbing gradually across several low ridges and gullies. At 0.5 mile the trail enters a side wash and then swings to the right (north) toward Fall Canyon. At 0.7 mile the use trail tops out above Fall Canyon, drops into the wide graveled wash, and vanishes after another 0.1 mile at the canyon mouth. At first the canyon is wide, up to 150 feet in places. At 1.3 miles the walls steepen and close in; dark shadows fill the bottom, adding to a feeling of intimacy. The canyon quickly opens to a huge amphitheater–alcove, bounded by sheer cliffs on the left, bending tightly to the right. At 1.5 miles a large rock sits in a wide bottom that opens to colorful bands of red, white, and gray on the cliff faces. Continue left up the main wash. The canyon narrows again at 1.8 miles, its sides pocketed with a myriad of ledges and small alcoves, only to open again with

the west rim soaring 1,000 feet overhead. At 2 miles a narrow side canyon enters from the left just above a massive boulder that blocks much of the wash. Continue to the right up the main wash next to an isolated rock pinnacle.

Soon the canyon narrows once more with rock overhangs reaching out above. At 2.2 miles colorful folded rock dramatizes the powerful forces that continue to shape this rugged landscape. The canyon squeezes to a gap of only 8 feet at 2.6 miles, widens, and then narrows again at 2.9 miles. A sheer 20-foot-high dry fall is reached at 3 miles. The fall cannot be safely or easily climbed, so this is a good turnaround point for an exhilarating 6-mile out-and-back exploration of Fall Canyon. To this point, the difficulty rating is moderate.

To continue up Fall Canyon, drop back down the wash less than 0.1 mile and look for rock cairns on the left (south) side (right side of the canyon going up). This bypass route around the fall should only be attempted by those with at least moderate rock-climbing skills and experience. Begin by climbing a steep but solid rock pitch to a well-defined use trail that angles above and around the right side of the fall. Exercise caution on the loose gravel directly above the canyon. Immediately above and beyond the fall, the canyon becomes extremely narrow, bounded by sheer cliffs, folded layers of rock, overhangs, and semicircular bends of smooth gray rock. There are a few short rock pitches that can be easily scrambled up.

At 3.2 miles the tight chasm opens to more distant cliffs, but the actual wash remains narrow. At 3.4 miles a massive boulder blocks most of the wash, with the easiest way around being to the left. Here the hardest part about turning around is turning around; every steep-walled bend entices further exploration. The gray-walled canyon, polished smooth by the action of water, is left at 3.5 miles with the valley opening to reddish rhyolite cliffs and peaks.

At 4.1 miles dramatic cliffs rise above steep slopes punctuated with jagged columns of dark rhyolite. Anywhere in this stretch provides a good turnaround point, but it is possible to continue climbing northward for another 4 miles to the head of the canyon, where the country opens up into low ridges, high plateaus, and open desert. Retrace your route to complete your exploration of this enchanting canyon.

Miles and Directions

0.0 Start at the trailhead at the mouth of Titus Canyon, behind the restroom.

0.7 The use trail meets the Fall Canyon wash.

0.8 Arrive at the mouth of Fall Canyon.

A hiker sits above a 20-foot-high dry fall 3 miles up Fall Canyon.

1.3	The canyon narrows dramatically.
2.9	Rock cairns mark a faint, scrambling use trail to the right that climbs above the dry fall.
3.0	Reach a 20-foot dry fall; turnaround point for the short hike.
3.1	The canyon narrows.
4.1	The canyon opens up to high peaks and ridges beyond.
8.0	Reach the head of the canyon.
16.0	Return to the trailhead from the longer hike.

32 Red Wall Canyon

Red Wall Canyon deserves its name. After crossing the open desert floor of Death Valley, this hike takes you into a rugged, brightly colored canyon in the Grapevine Mountains. The cool shadows of the deep canyon provide a respite from the glare of the desert outside.

See map on page 108.
Start: About 36 miles north of Furnace Creek.
Distance: 7 miles out and back.
Approximate hiking time: 2 to 3 hours.
Difficulty: Moderate.

Trail surface: Sandy rocky wash, gravel canyon floor.
Seasons: October through April.
USGS topo map: Fall Canyon-CA (1:24,000).
Trail contact: Furnace Creek Visitor Center & Museum (see appendix D).

Finding the trailhead: The main wash of the alluvial fan is 35.5 miles north of Furnace Creek, 17.4 miles south of Scotty's Castle, and 14.1 miles south of the Grapevine Ranger Station. The hike takes off from Scotty's Castle Road, 3.8 miles north of the Titus Canyon Road exit, and heads northeast across 3 miles of sloping desert alluvial fan to the mouth of Red Wall Canyon.

The Hike

Although rock-climbing skills are needed to proceed beyond a dry waterfall 0.5 mile up the canyon, this hike provides delightful vistas in the lower canyon region for the casual hiker. The trip can also be extended to a point-to-point excursion (with a car shuttle) by hiking from Red Wall Canyon to the Titus Canyon parking area, 3.5 miles to the south.

The approach to the canyon via the alluvial fan is not particularly challenging, but it is certainly not easy! The easiest hiking is on the dark desert pavement of the old alluvial fan. The wash route changes directions with its tributaries, so it's necessary to cut from wash to wash to maintain the route to the canyon mouth. Above the wash, the sections of smoother varnished desert pavement provide some respite,

The entrance to Red Wall Canyon.

but these sections are brief, interspersed with sections of cobbled, bouldered, and eroded washbeds.

The canyon mouth opens to the northwest; except for the red/black wall contrast, it is nearly hidden in the cliff faces. The canyon, which looked so narrow or invisible during the approach, is surprisingly wide, at least 50 yards from wall to wall. At the entrance, the north wall is a sheer red cliff face, while the south side is a black slope. The canyon takes a sharp turn to the north 0.2 mile farther, and suddenly the Red Wall towers 400 feet above you on the right. A narrow S-curve brings you to another red wall, now on your left. A short distance farther an even redder wall appears. The red walls, alternating with the black, provide a blast of sharp color on the beige desert palette.

At mile 0.4 in the canyon, water-sculpted narrows enclose an easily climbed low dry fall. Just beyond this obstacle is the 20-foot dry fall that blocks the canyon to all but seasoned rock climbers. Don't trust the knotted rope hanging at the dry fall. Using ropes of unknown origin, age, or strength is never recommended. So this is a good turnaround or lunch spot.

In Red Wall the variety of canyon architecture lures you onward as the canyon is constantly bending out of sight. Only upon turning around for the hike back are you aware of the elevation gained (800 feet in 0.5 mile). The descent from the dry fall provides numerous vistas of Death Valley in the distance.

The sharp slope of the canyon floor and its heavy gravel surface both indicate that this is a relatively young canyon. There is still a lot of erosive energy in the uplifting Amargosa Range, of which these Grapevine Mountains are a part.

Miles and Directions

0.0 From whatever point on Scotty's Castle Road you select, aim for the Grapevine Mountains. The canyon mouth is where the red and black rock faces meet. The alluvial fan emerging from the canyon forms a distinct triangle. Head up this alluvial fan, cross-country or via one of the washes.

3.0 Enter the canyon.

3.5 A 20-foot dry fall blocks the canyon. The use of the knotted rope of unknown age and origin is not recommended for scaling the fall.

7.0 Return to the trailhead by the same route.

Option: For the avid desert hiker, another approach (or exit) for the Red Wall hike is from the Titus Canyon/Fall Canyon trailhead. From the Red Wall Canyon mouth, you can see the most efficient pathway across the fan and the ridges to the south. Since the finger ridges hide sharply eroded dropoffs, aim for their lower western edges in your southward hike. A faint use trail is intermittent on this cross-country hike, visible only on the desert pavement ridges, and marked by a few cairns.

Like all rugged cross-country journeys, this hike does not allow a direct line. Detours are constantly required for steep ridges, deep washes, and high alluvial plateaus. Eroded cliffs of volcanic-ash badlands obstruct the shortest distance from Red Wall to Titus. With neither shade nor cover, this trip should only be undertaken with plenty of water.

In the midst of a busy section of the park, this canyon-to-canyon hike, 2 miles from the road below, provides a taste of true desert travel. The silence of the desert surrounds you. The difficulties of desert hiking abound. From your 1,000-foot elevation, you enjoy sweeping views of the valley below as well as the Grapevines above. Your destination dances in the distance as both Fall and Titus Canyons at once appear close but don't get any closer! A cooperative partner can let you off at the alluvial fan on the Grapevine Road then meet you at the Titus parking area several hours later. The 8.5-mile hike south to Titus takes twice as long (three to four hours) as the direct hike up the fan, but it is worth the effort.

33 Ubehebe Peak

Ubehebe Peak is one of the few Death Valley peaks largely accessible by trail. The steep out-and-back hike leads to a remote peak in the southern Last Chance Range from which you will enjoy spectacular views of surrounding basin and range country.

Start: About 81 miles northwest of Furnace Creek.
Distance: 6.2 miles out and back.
Approximate hiking time: 3 to 5 hours.
Difficulty: Strenuous.
Trail surface: Clear rocky trail, changing to good, then to primitive, and finally to no trail for the final 0.4 mile to the summit.

Seasons: October through June.
USGS topo map: Ubehebe Peak-CA (1:24,000).
Trail contact: Furnace Creek Visitor Center & Museum (see appendix D).

Finding the trailhead: From the junction of Scotty's Castle Road and Ubehebe Crater Road in the northeastern corner of the park, head northwest on the paved Ubehebe Crater Road. The pavement ends after 5.3 miles at the turnoff to Ubehebe Crater. Continue south on the washboard dirt Racetrack Valley Road 19.7 miles to Teakettle Junction. Here Racetrack Valley Road turns right; continue to follow it another 5.7 miles to the Grandstand parking area, which is opposite the "grandstand" of gray rocks in the dry lake bed east of the road. The trail heads west from the parking area toward the prominent Ubehebe Peak.

The Hike

Before climbing Ubehebe Peak, a short 1-mile round-trip hike east to the Grandstand is a worthwhile warm-up and also provides a good perspective on your journey to the top of Ubehebe Peak. From the Grandstand, a pre-climb visual orientation involves identifying Ubehebe Peak on the left with your route going up the east face of the north peak, then around the back side into the prominent notch, then left up the skyline to the peak.

The Grandstand is a large 70-foot-high mound of gray rocks rising in stark contrast to the surrounding white flatness of the Racetrack playa, or dry lake bed. For added perspective, walk around the Grandstand, then scramble up some of the large boulders. The Grandstand can be easily climbed 40 to 50 feet above the playa. Be on the lookout for the tracks of "moving rocks" streaked across the lake-bed sediment. The mystery of these mobile rocks is heightened by the fact that no one has ever seen them move. Most likely the rocks are swept by powerful winds when the lake bed is slickened by heavy rain. If time allows upon completion of the peak climb, drive south from the Grandstand another 2 miles. Walk to the east toward the base of Peak 4,560. This is where you will find the best view of the mysterious trails of the moving rocks. Please do not walk on the Racetrack if it is wet or muddy.

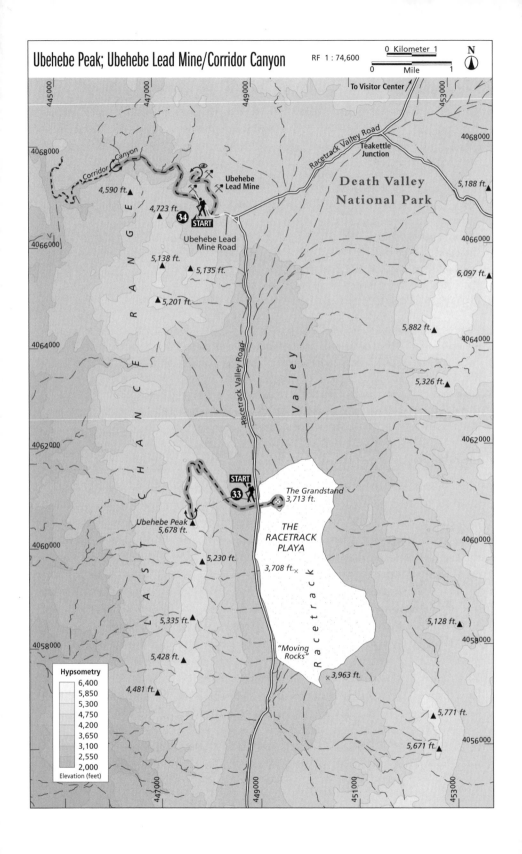

Ubehebe Peak; Ubehebe Lead Mine/Corridor Canyon

RF 1 : 74,600

0 Kilometer 1

0 Mile 1

N

To Visitor Center

445000 447000 449000 453000

4068000

Racetrack Valley Road

Teakettle Junction

4068000

Corridor Canyon

4,590 ft. ▲

Ubehebe Lead Mine

Death Valley National Park

5,188 ft. ▲

4,723 ft. ▲

34 START

Ubehebe Lead Mine Road

L A S T   C H A N C E   R A N G E

4066000

5,138 ft. ▲

▲ 5,135 ft.

6,097 ft. ▲

4066000

▲ 5,201 ft.

Racetrack Valley Road

Racetrack   Valley

5,882 ft. ▲

4064000

4064000

5,326 ft. ▲

4062000

4062000

START 33

The Grandstand 3,713 ft.

Ubehebe Peak 5,678 ft. ▲

THE RACETRACK PLAYA

4060000

▲ 5,230 ft.

3,708 ft. ×

4060000

R a c e t r a c k

5,128 ft. ▲

5,335 ft. ▲

"Moving Rocks"

5,428 ft. ▲

× 3,963 ft.

4058000

4058000

Hypsometry

6,400
5,850
5,300
4,750
4,200
3,650
3,100
2,550
2,000

Elevation (feet)

4,481 ft. ▲

5,771 ft. ▲

5,671 ft. ▲

4056000

447000 449000 451000 453000

Ubehebe Peak (right) towers over the playa (dry lake bed) far below.

Be sure to carry sufficient water for this high, dry desert peak climb. The clear trail, originally an old mining path, begins by ascending gradually to the northwest up an alluvial fan clothed with desert trumpets and creosote bushes. Within 0.5 mile the trail begins a long series of steep switchbacks up the east face of the 5,519-foot north peak. This imposing buttress is made even more impressive with broken cliffs of desert varnish. After climbing nearly 1,200 feet in 1.8 miles, the trail reaches the north ridge of the peak, just after passing an outcropping of limestone where the blue-green copper of malachite rock lines a shallow mine digging. From this point, a trail takes off to the right, ending after 0.1 mile at an overlook above an old mine entrance. The summit of Ubehebe Peak can be seen in the distance beyond the north peak, which rises directly above.

Continue up the left-hand trail, which climbs steeply up the ridge through the rocks to 5,160 feet at 2 miles. The trail then wraps around the west side of the mountain, reaching an elevation of 5,440 feet at 2.4 miles. From here on, the trail becomes rougher and more faint, compensated somewhat by stupendous views of the playa to the southeast. The trail then drops for another 0.2 mile to the 5,220-foot saddle between the two peaks. Any resemblance to a trail ends at the saddle, which is a good turnaround point for those not wishing to scramble the steep rocky ridge another 0.4 mile and 460 vertical feet to Ubehebe Peak.

To attain the summit, climb southward straight up the rugged spine of the north ridge. Much of this route is marked by rock cairns. There are no technical sections, but care must be exercised in negotiating narrow chutes around steep rock faces. The quartz granite top of 5,678-foot Ubehebe Peak contains a summit register and is marked by a wooden triangle. Although narrow, there are lots of ideal sitting spots upon which to relax and soak up the incredible 360-degree vista.

The Saline Valley lies 4,500 feet below to the west. Beyond is the soaring 10,000-foot crest of the Inyo Mountains with the even higher Sierra Nevada looming farther to the west. The crown of Death Valley—lofty Telescope Peak—can be seen to the southeast, along with the vast wooded plateau of Hunter Mountain. Perhaps most impressive is the eagle's-eye view of the gleaming white Racetrack playa encircling the tiny dark specks of the Grandstand far below.

Miles and Directions

0.0 Start from the trailhead at the Grandstand parking area on the Racetrack Valley Road.

1.8 The trail switchbacks to the north ridge of the peak. Where the trail splits, stay left.

2.4 The trail reaches a ridge on the west side of the mountain, becoming rougher and more faint.

2.7 The trail drops to a saddle between the two peaks. Begin the route-finding segment to the peak.

3.1 Reach Ubehebe Peak (5,678 feet).

6.2 Return to the trailhead.

34 Ubehebe Lead Mine/Corridor Canyon

This exploration of a historic mine site with a tram will appeal to mining and history buffs. The longer leg in Corridor Canyon will enchant those who appreciate excellent vistas of cliffs and mountains.

See map on page 116.
Start: About 76 miles northwest of Furnace Creek.
Distance: 6 miles out and back.
Approximate hiking time: 4 hours.
Difficulty: Moderate.

Trail surface: Dirt path to mine; clear wash in canyon.
Seasons: October through March.
USGS topo maps: Ubehebe Peak-CA and Teakettle Junction-CA (1:24,000).
Trail contact: Furnace Creek Visitor Center & Museum (see appendix D).

Finding the trailhead: From Grapevine Junction, take Ubehebe Crater Road northwest 5.5 miles to the end of the pavement and the sign for Racetrack Valley Road. Turn right onto Racetrack Valley Road. Four-wheel drive is recommended but under normal weather conditions is unnecessary. Racetrack Valley Road is severely washboarded but contains no other obstacles as far as the Racetrack. Go south on Racetrack Valley Road 19.6 miles to Teakettle Junction. Bear right and continue 2.2 miles to the right turn to Ubehebe Lead Mine Road (signed). The dirt road leads 0.7 mile to the parking area at the mine site.

The Hike

The Ubehebe Mine has a lengthy history, beginning in 1875 when copper ore was found here. The copper mine was not fully developed until early in the twentieth century, but the profitable ore was soon depleted. In 1908 lead mining began and continued until 1928. Ubehebe Mine had another renaissance in the 1940s as a zinc mine. Mining activity came to an end in 1951.

After all this mining it is not surprising to find a plethora of mining artifacts in the valley and in the hills above. A miner's house is still standing. Its door and windows ajar, stripped of its plumbing (the range lies outside), it is a well-preserved remnant of its midcentury inhabitants. Remember that it may be unwise to enter deserted buildings due to deer mice and hanta virus.

In the wash above there are other traces of crude dwellings of miners. Stacked stone walls are still in place. The men worked inside rock walls by day and slept in them at night. Rusty debris and small, level tent sites are scattered about. The usual squeaky bedspring (burned and rusted) lies amid the creosote bushes. This is an appropriate place to pause and contemplate the bustle of activity and spirit of optimism that must have prevailed in this mining valley in its various heydays.

Below the housing area sits the ore chute, with rail tracks still leading from a mine opening. The area looks like it had been deserted only a year ago. The sagging

The chute at the Ubehebe Lead Mine.

old tram cable still hangs from the tower atop the hill to the valley floor. Unsecured mine openings dot the hillside. Although the National Park Service has not posted its usual warning sign, do not get close to the mines; the tram should also be given a wide berth.

The hike up the trail to the overlook gives you a magnificent aerial view of the mine encampment and the rolling hills of the Last Chance Range. Mine openings proliferate like rodent burrows. The rust-colored rock and earth in piles at each opening give the mining operations an eerie fresh appearance, as if the work here just stopped yesterday instead of 60 or 100 years ago. Numerous wooden posts mark the mountainside along the trail to designate claims of long-gone prospectors. Crossing carefully beneath the hilltop tram tower, you arrive at trail's end and a view westward of winding Corridor Canyon.

For this 5-mile out-and-back leg into Corridor Canyon, start at the mine chute and drop down the wide and graveled wash to the head of the canyon, generally westward. At 0.3 mile a tantalizing narrow stair-step chute of a canyon enters from

the left, inviting exploration—although large boulders may prevent you from getting very far.

At about 1 mile impressive cliff walls soar high to the left, whereas the right side is marked by folded rock layers altered by fault lines. Below, as the canyon turns left, are colorful bands of rock. The cliffs are pockmarked with caverns and other small openings, some of which serve as active dens for animals.

The canyon is unique in that it provides both a closed-in experience as well as far distant vistas of cliffs, overshadowed by even higher cliff layers beyond, opening to expansive views of adjacent and faraway mountains. Hike another 1.5 miles in the wide wash before turning around and retracing your steps.

Miles and Directions

Mine:

0.0–0.1 Back up the road from the miner's shack, on the north side by a low stone wall, the trail leads up the hillside.

0.4 There's a tram cable tower at the hilltop.

0.5 Enjoy the view at the overlook.

1.0 Return to the trailhead by the same route.

Canyon:

0.0 At the mine chute, head west down the wash.

0.3 The chute canyon enters from the left.

1.0 View dramatic cliffs, continuing in the canyon until you decide to turn around at one of various turnaround points.

2.5 By this point you've seen what makes this canyon special. For more of the same, you could continue as much as 2.5 miles more.

5.0 Retrace your steps to the parking area.

35 Ubehebe and Little Hebe Craters

These volcanic craters are a fascinating geology lesson on the forces that helped form Death Valley. A short loop hike around the large Ubehebe Crater and the several smaller ones enables you to witness the complex erosion patterns that have occurred since the craters' birth.

Start: About 51 miles north of Furnace Creek.
Distance: 1.5-mile loop.
Approximate hiking time: 1 to 2 hours.
Difficulty: Easy; moderate to the bottom of the crater.
Trail surface: Volcanic cinder.

Seasons: Late October through April.
USGS topo map: Ubehebe Crater-CA (1:24,000).
Trail contact: Furnace Creek Visitor Center & Museum (see appendix D).

Finding the trailhead: From the Grapevine Junction of Scotty's Castle Road and Ubehebe Crater Road, 45 miles north of Furnace Creek, take Ubehebe Crater Road northwest. Drive 5.7 miles to the Ubehebe Crater parking area for the Ubehebe Crater/Little Hebe Crater trailhead. The parking area is on the eastern side on the one-way loop of paved road at the end of Ubehebe Crater Road.

The Hike

The volcanic region at the north end of the Cottonwood Mountains, near Scotty's Castle, is evidence of recent cataclysmic events in Death Valley, geologically speaking. The huge Ubehebe Crater was created around 3,000 years ago when magma heated groundwater and the pressure from the resulting steam blew the overlying rock away. This explosion covered 6 square miles of desert with volcanic debris 150 feet deep. Called a maar volcano by geologists, Ubehebe is a crater without a cone. The rim has been eroding ever since the explosion, gradually filling the crater with alluvial fans.

Little Hebe, directly south, is much younger. Having exploded about 300 to 500 years ago, it is one of the newest geologic features of Death Valley. Little Hebe's rim is neat and well defined, exhibiting little of the erosion that has reduced Ubehebe's edge.

Pausing at the parking lot to read the information on the board and glancing at these monstrous holes in the earth might seem sufficient, but hiking all the way around this monumental display of volcanic power provides a much better understanding of the dimensions of the Ubehebe complex.

The first fourth of the hike takes you along the rim of the main crater. The size of the hole is overpowering. It is almost 0.5 mile across from rim to rim. Alluvial fans have formed on the walls as the rains tear down the crater's edges.

The sharply defined rim of Little Hebe Crater is evidence of its youth, geologically speaking.

In the vicinity of Ubehebe, there are as many as twelve additional craters, all examples of more maar activity. You will see numerous craters in various stages of eroding deterioration. Little Hebe stands out as a jewel of a crater. Neat and trim, this volcanic chasm is only 200 yards across. The younger, fresher rim has barely begun to weather. Volcanic materials are very durable. Clearly visible on the walls of Little Hebe are the layers beneath the earth's surface. Especially noticeable is a thick layer of viscous lava that had oozed from the earth's interior prior to the explosion of Little Hebe.

After the tour around Little Hebe, continue your hike around the main crater, which seems even larger after visiting its younger neighbor. A well-defined trail leads around Ubehebe. At 1.3 miles pass the trail that slopes down into the crater—see the option below. The volcanic cinder trail descends nearly 500 feet to the floor of the crater, where creosote bushes flourish. After major rainstorms the crater also features a small lake. Most of the time it is very dry.

The power of nature to modify the terrain via volcanic action stands in sharp contrast with the more gradual erosive forces that are demonstrated elsewhere in

Ubehebe and Little Hebe Craters

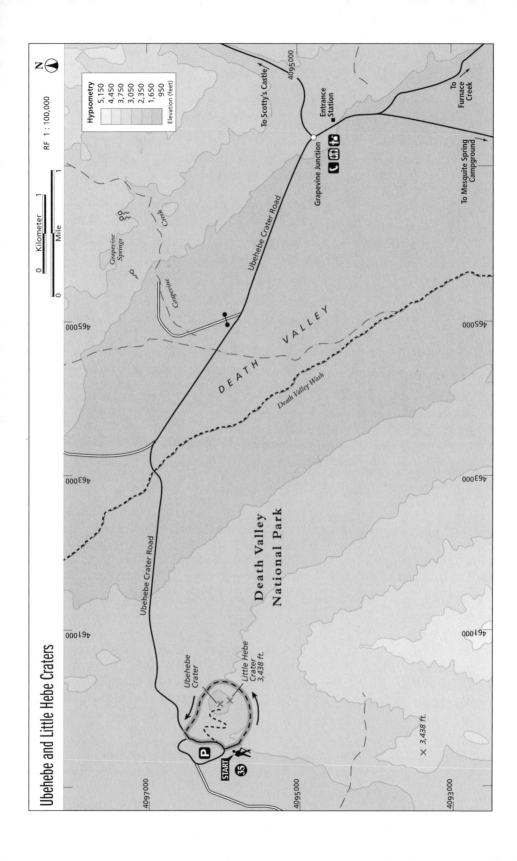

Death Valley. The earth has not finished rearranging its surface here in Death Valley. The forces that created Ubehebe and Little Hebe are merely dormant, not dead.

Miles and Directions

0.0 The trail goes south of the information board at the parking area.

0.1–0.3 The trail climbs—bear left at the Y. The trail to the right is eroding on both sides and becoming hazardous.

0.4 Arrive at a maze of use trails on a small plateau between craters. A sign directs you to Little Hebe, directly south. Follow the trail around Little Hebe.

0.7 Back at the intersection, continue to hike around the large Ubehebe Crater.

1.5 Return to the trailhead.

Option: The 0.6-mile out and back to the bottom of the crater is a breathtaking outing into the earth. At the bottom you can imagine the force that blew off the earth to leave such a hole. The climb back to the parking area requires some exertion due to the skidding quality of the volcanic cinders.

36 Eureka Dunes

In a remote desert valley, against the scenic backdrop of the colorful Last Chance Mountains, lie the Eureka Dunes. These are the tallest sand dunes in California and the second-highest in all of North America, although their constantly shifting nature would make that tough to measure. Your cross-country walk to their summit will be a soft sandy stroll.

Start: About 90 miles north of Furnace Creek.
Distance: 3-mile loop.
Approximate hiking time: 2 hours.
Difficulty: Moderate.
Trail surface: All-sand cross-country route.

Seasons: October through April.
USGS topo map: Last Chance Range Southwest-CA (1:24,000).
Trail contact: Furnace Creek Visitor Center & Museum (see appendix D).

Finding the trailhead: From the south, take Scotty's Castle Road to Grapevine Junction and proceed northwest on Ubehebe Crater Road for 2.8 miles to Big Pine Road, which is also known as North Entrance Highway and Death Valley Road. The turnoff is signed EUREKA DUNES 45 MILES. Turn north onto the washboard, graded gravel Big Pine Road and drive 34 miles to South Eureka Valley Road, which is the road to the Eureka Dunes. Turn left (south) onto this road and drive 10 miles to the end-of-the-road picnic/parking area near the base of the dunes. From the north, Eureka Dunes can be reached from Big Pine via 28 miles of paved road and 11 miles of graded dirt road to South Eureka Valley Road. Turn right (south) and follow the narrow road for the final 10 miles to the camping and parking areas just north of the dunes.

The multibanded Last Chance Mountains provide a colorful backdrop to the 3,480-foot summit of the Eureka Dunes.

The Hike

The Eureka Dunes are a fascinating island of sand in a desert sea, within the recently expanded northern portion of the park. From a distance this 1-by-3-mile mountain of sand seems to hover over the remote Eureka Valley floor. Although not extensive, these dunes are the tallest in California and the second-tallest in North America after the Great Sand Dunes in Colorado. From the dry lake bed at their western edge, the Eureka Dunes rise abruptly more than 600 feet. Equally impressive is the sheer face of the Last Chance Mountains to the immediate east, with their colored striped bands of pink, black, and gray limestone.

If the sand here is completely dry, you may hear one of the most unusual sounds in the desert: singing sand. When the sand cascades down the steepest pitch of the highest dune, a rumbling sound comparable to the bass note of a pipe organ emanates from the sand. No one knows exactly why this happens, but the friction of smooth-textured sand grains sliding against each other probably has something to do with it.

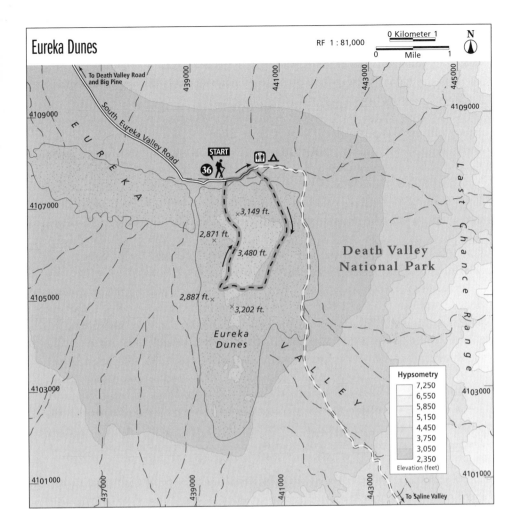

These dunes receive more moisture than others in the park because they are positioned at the western foot of a high mountain range that intercepts passing storms. The isolation of the Eureka Dunes, far from any other dunes, has resulted in endemic species of animals and plants found nowhere else. For example, there are five species of beetles and three plants that have their entire range limited to these lofty mounds.

The three endemic plant species are shining locoweed, a candidate for endangered species listing, Eureka dune grass, and Eureka evening primrose, the latter two of which are listed as endangered species under the federal Endangered Species Act. The camping area and trailhead were recently moved off of the dunes to protect these species. Shining locoweed is a hummock-forming plant with root nodules that fix nitrogen from the air, a vital plant nutrient not available in the sand. When wind-blown sand covers the leafy flower shoots of the Eureka evening primrose, a new rosette of leaves forms at the tip. Large, white flowers bloom at night so that moths and other pollinators can avoid daytime heat. Usually Eureka dune grass is the only plant on the higher slopes of the dunes. Its thick roots hold shifting sand, forming hummocks. Stiff, spiny leaf tips discourage herbivores.

The Eureka Dunes are a small, ecologically unique place requiring our special care. Camp and keep vehicles a good distance from the base of the dunes, which is where most of the endemic plants and animals live. If possible, walk where others have in order to concentrate the impact away from pristine areas.

There are two basic choices for climbing the dunes, which can be hard work at times in the loose, shifting sand. The most direct route for the 600-plus-foot climb to the top is a 1.5-mile straight-up-and-back route by way of a series of knife ridges. Because of the long driving distance to the trailhead, a somewhat longer 3-mile loop is your better choice. In so choosing, you'll gain more intimacy with the dunes and their majestic Last Chance Mountains backdrop.

From the parking/camping area, head east cross-country along the base of the dunes toward the color-banded Last Chance Mountains, which rise an impressive 4,000 feet above the Eureka Valley floor. Hiking along the base provides a constantly changing perspective of this unusual landscape as well as a good warm-up for climbing the steep backside of the dunes. A profusion of animal tracks will appear as well as the circular paths of grass tips in the sand from the ever-changing wind.

At 0.8 mile the initial flat stretch becomes laced with up-and-down gullies, with volcanic "bombs" embedded in the sand. At this point begin curving around the base of the dunes to the right (south). This wonderfully wide-open trek stands in startling contrast to the closed-in feeling one gets when exploring the deep canyons of Death Valley.

At around 1.5 miles begin climbing westward up any one of the several narrow knife-edge sand ridges that converge at the apex of the dunes. A vertical gain of about 600 feet to the 3,480-foot high point is spread over about 0.7 mile, with most of the climb during the final 0.2 mile. The dry lake bed, expansive Eureka Valley, colorful Last Chance Range, and the dunes themselves combine to form a stunning 360-degree panorama. To complete the 3-mile loop, continue back down along narrow ridges and steep scooped-out bowls of sand in a north to northwesterly direction to the trailhead.

Miles and Directions

0.0 Start from the trailhead located at the picnic tables/parking area.

1.5 Begin climbing up the west side of the dunes.

2.2 Reach the top of the dunes.

3.0 Complete the loop back to the trailhead.

Afterword

As seasoned hikers accustomed to the high snowy mountains of the Northern Rockies, we were excited when the idea of exploring some of the California desert was presented to us. It would be hard to find two more disparate regions—the California desert and the Northern Rockies—within the lower forty-eight. We viewed the opportunity to learn more about such a different ecosystem as a tremendous challenge. And we foresaw many interim challenges along the way, such as the challenge of truly getting to know this splendid country and its hidden treasures beyond the roads. There would be the challenges of climbing rugged peaks, of safely traversing vast expanses of open desert, of navigating across alluvial fans to secluded canyons, of learning enough about the interconnected web of desert geology, flora, and fauna to be able to interpret some of its wonders for others to appreciate. These beckoned to us from blank spots on the park map.

But we each face a far greater challenge: the challenge of wilderness stewardship, which must be shared by all who venture into the wilderness of Death Valley and California's other desert parks.

Wilderness stewardship can take many forms, from political advocacy to a zero-impact hiking and camping ethic to quietly setting the example of respect for wild country for others to follow. The political concessions that eventually brought about passage of the long-awaited California Desert Protection Act have been made. Boundaries were gerrymandered, exclusions made, and nonconforming uses grandfathered. Still, the wilderness and park lines that have been drawn in Death Valley National Park represent a tremendous step forward in the ongoing battle to save what little remains of our diminishing wilderness heritage.

But drawing lines is only the first step. Now, the great challenge is to take care of what we have. We can each demonstrate this care every time we set out on a hike. It comes down to respect for the untamed but fragile desert, for those wild creatures who have no place else to live, for other visitors, and for those yet unborn who will retrace our hikes into the next century and beyond.

We will be judged not by the mountains we climb but by what we pass on to others in an unimpaired condition. Happy hiking, and may your trails be clear with the wind and sun at your back.

Appendix A: Our Favorite Hikes

Mountains

Telescope Peak (18) Central peak with magnificent view

Open Desert

Eureka Dunes (36) Highest dunes in North America, backdrop of Last Chance Range

Canyons

Marble Canyon (25) Twisting walls with varied stripes and colors
Fall Canyon (31) Sheer walls above narrow canyon

Waterfalls and Streams

Surprise Canyon to Panamint City (17) Spring-fed stream, chutes
Darwin Falls (23) Hideaway canyon with compound falls

Interpretive Nature Trails

Golden Canyon/Gower Gulch Loop (9) Geology of Death Valley
Salt Creek Interpretive Trail (29) Geologic changes and pupfish

Prehistory and History

Hungry Bill's Ranch/Johnson Canyon (16) Farm of 1880s

Mines and Mills

Ashford Canyon/Mine (2) Numerous mine buildings in scenic canyon
Keane Wonder Mine (13) Extraordinary tramway, mine, and mill

Appendix B: Recommended Equipment

Use the following checklists as you assemble your gear for hiking the California desert.

Day Hike

- ❏ sturdy, well-broken-in, light- to medium-weight hiking boots
- ❏ broad-brimmed hat, which must be windproof
- ❏ long-sleeved shirt for sun protection
- ❏ long pants for protection against sun and brush
- ❏ water: two quarts to one gallon/day (depending on season), in sturdy screw-top plastic containers
- ❏ large-scale topo map and compass (adjusted for magnetic declination)
- ❏ whistle, mirror, and matches (for emergency signals)
- ❏ flashlight (in case your hike takes longer than you expect)
- ❏ sunblock and lip sunscreen
- ❏ insect repellent (in season)
- ❏ pocketknife
- ❏ small first-aid kit: tweezers, bandages, antiseptic, moleskin, snakebite extractor kit
- ❏ bee sting kit (over-the-counter antihistamine or epinephrine by prescription) as needed for the season
- ❏ windbreaker (or rain gear in season)
- ❏ lunch or snack, with baggie for your trash
- ❏ toilet paper, with a plastic zipper bag to pack it out
- ❏ your FalconGuide

Optional gear
- ❏ camera and film
- ❏ binoculars
- ❏ bird and plant guidebooks
- ❏ notebook and pen/pencil

Winter High-Country Trips

All of the above, plus:
- ❏ gaiters
- ❏ warm ski-type hat and gloves
- ❏ warm jacket

Backpacking Trips/Overnights

All of the above, plus:

- ☐ backpack (internal or external frame)
- ☐ more water (at least a gallon a day, plus extra for cooking—cache or carry)
- ☐ clothing for the season
- ☐ sleeping bag and pad
- ☐ tent with fly
- ☐ toiletries
- ☐ stove with fuel bottle and repair kit
- ☐ pot, bowl, cup, and eating utensils
- ☐ food (freeze-dried meals require extra water)
- ☐ water filter designed and approved for backcountry use (if the route passes a water source)
- ☐ nylon cord (50 to 100 feet for hanging food, drying clothes, etc.)
- ☐ additional plastic bags for carrying out trash

Appendix C: Other Information Sources and Maps

Natural History Association

Death Valley Natural History Association
P.O. Box 188
Death Valley, CA 92328
(800) 478–8564
Web site: www.deathvalleydays.com/dvnha

The association is a nonprofit membership organization dedicated to the preservation and interpretation of the natural and human history of the park. Membership benefits include book discounts, educational programs, and periodic newsletters.

Other Handy Maps

Although the "At a Glance" chart lists only the detailed 7.5-minute topographic maps for each hike, the natural history association also sells additional maps that are indispensable for overall trip planning and for navigating around the park to and between hikes. These recommended maps are:

Death Valley National Park

- Death Valley National Park topographic backcountry and hiking map, 1:160,000 scale, published by National Geographic/Trails Illustrated
- AAA map of Death Valley National Park published by the Automobile Club of Southern California

Appendix D: Park Management Agencies

Furnace Creek Visitor Center and Museum
Furnace Creek Resort Area on California Highway 190
Death Valley National Park
(760) 786–3200
(Open year-round 8:00 A.M. to 5:00 P.M.)
Camping reservations, Destinet; (800) 365–CAMP (2267)
Web site: www.nps.gov/deva

Scotty's Castle Visitor Center and Museum
North end of DVNP on Nevada State Route 267
Death Valley National Park
(760) 786–2392
(Open year-round 8:30 A.M. to 5:00 P.M.)

Beatty Information Center
Beatty, Nevada, on U.S. Highway 95
Death Valley National Park
(775) 553–2200
(Open year-round)

For information about wilderness and other public lands adjacent to the park, contact:
Bureau of Land Management
California Desert District
6221 Box Springs Boulevard
Riverside, CA 92507
(951) 697–5200
Web site: www.californiadesert.gov

Index

About the Authors

Polly and Bill Cunningham are married partners on the long trail of life. Polly, formerly a history teacher in St. Louis, Missouri, now makes her home with Bill in Choteau, Montana. She is pursuing multiple careers as a freelance writer and wilderness guide and working with the elderly. Polly has hiked and backpacked extensively throughout many parts of the country.

Bill is a lifelong "Wildernut," as a conservation activist, backpacking outfitter, and former wilderness field studies instructor. During the 1970s and 1980s he was a field rep for The Wilderness Society and Montana Wilderness Association. Bill has written several books, including *Wild Montana,* published by Falcon Press in 1995, along with numerous articles about wilderness areas based on his extensive personal exploration.

In addition to *Hiking Death Valley National Park,* Polly and Bill have coauthored several other FalconGuide books, including *Wild Utah* (1998), *Hiking New Mexico's Gila Wilderness* (1999), *Hiking New Mexico's Aldo Leopold Wilderness* (2002), and *Hiking California's Desert Parks* (2006).

Decades ago both Bill and Polly lived in California close to the desert—Bill in Bakersfield and Polly in San Diego. They enjoyed renewing their ties with California while exploring Death Valley National Park for this book. Months of driving, camping, and hiking, with laptop and camera, have increased their enthusiasm for California's desert wilderness. They want others to have as much fun exploring this fabulously wide-open country as they did.

Authors Polly and Bill Cunningham